THE BIG BOOK OF BIBLE TRUTHS 1

THE BIG BOOK OF BIBLE TRUTHS 1

SINCLAIR B. FERGUSON

CF4·K

The Big Book of Bible Truths 1
ISBN: 978-1-84550-371-0
© 2008 Sinclair B Ferguson
Published in 2008 by Christian Focus Publications, Geanies House, Fearn, Tain, Ross-shire, IV20 1TW,
Great Britain.
www.christianfocus.com
Cover design by: Daniel van Straaten
Printed by: Bell and Bain
All rights reserved. No part of this publication may be reproduced, stored in a retrieval system, or transmitted, in any form, by any means, electronic, mechanical, photocopying, recording or otherwise without the prior permission of the publisher or a licence permitting restricted copying. In the U.K. such licences are issued by the Copyright Licensing Agency, Saffron House, 6-10 Kirby Street, London, EC1 8TS. www.cla.co.uk

---

Remembering

IAN MACDOUGALL

who enjoyed these stories,
recorded them,
and
made this book possible.

Contents

Running the Race 6
Belonging to Jesus 8
What is a Christian? 10
Nicknames 12
How to be Patient 14
The Heart...16
Don't be a Coward 18
Just do it!...20
Don't Look Back 22
A Wicked Tongue 24
Growing Up 26
Follow the Way 28
Paul Casts His Vote 30
Oxy-what? 32
Nicodemus 34
An Ethiopian Visitor 36
Get in a Time Machine 38
Paul in Trouble..40
David's Big Three 42
A Man Born Blind 44
Judas...46
On God's Side 48
Paul and Barnabas..50
Who do you Want? 52
Moth Burgers 54
The Bible 56
Famous Last Words 58

RUNNING THE RACE

The Christian Race

If you run in a race it can be hard going and very tiring! The Bible tells us that the Christian life is like a long race.

In Hebrews, Chapter 11, we read about Moses and Daniel. Moses suffered a great deal. Pharaoh was against him. Even his own Hebrew people criticised him. Daniel was thrown into a lion's den because he worshipped the one true God. His friends, Shadrach, Meshach and Abednego, were put in a fiery furnace because they would not worship the king's statue. They wanted to trust in the Lord and to serve him.

Eric Liddell was a famous athlete. In 1924 he won a gold medal in the Olympic games, but his most important race was the Christian race. He ran in this race because he loved the Lord Jesus. Eric went to China as a missionary and he died there. He ran the Christian race right to the end. It was hard at times, but he knew the Lord Jesus was with him.

You may feel that you are running this race all on your own. Perhaps there are no other Christians in your school. Maybe you are the only one in your family who loves Jesus? But remember this, all over the world there are millions of people who are following Jesus. They are running the Christian race, just like you, because it is the greatest race in the world.

READ: Hebrews 12: 1–2.

LESSON: The Bible tells us that following Jesus is like a race. Today's story tells us what it means to run for Jesus. This will help us to understand why the Christian life is like a race.

An Obstacle Race

If we run the Christian race we need to get rid of things that hold us back. These are obstacles. Hebrews, Chapter 12 tells us to throw away the things that keep us from following Jesus. Would you run in a race with a heavy rucksack on your back? Of course not! Well – just as there are things that make you slow down in a running race – there are things that get in the way in the Christian race too.

One of these things is greed. Do you spend lots of time thinking about the things that you want your parents to get you? We need to get rid of greed.

Lies, bad temper and pride hold us back too. We can't run the Christian race if we hold on to these things. The good news is that the Lord Jesus promises to help us get rid of them if we ask him. It may not be easy, but the Lord Jesus will help us so that we can run the Christian race and follow him.

A Marathon Race

A marathon race is twenty-six miles. It is the longest of all the races in the Olympic games. It commemorates a man who ran a long way to Athens in order to tell the people that their army had defeated the Persians at the Battle of Marathon.

Following Jesus is like a marathon. That is why we need to have the Holy Spirit to help us keep going. There will be times when we don't have the strength to keep going. But the Lord Jesus says, 'When you are weak, I will come and make you strong'.

A Prize Race

There are prizes for everybody who runs in the Christian race. We are told to keep our eyes on the finishing tape. One day the Christian race will be over at the end of our life on earth. But when we arrive at the finishing tape Jesus will be there to greet us. He will have a prize for us.

Part of this prize will be that Jesus will give us his own special name (Revelation 2: 17)! It will be the greatest prize in the world!

Let's run to get that prize. Jesus will help us all the way.

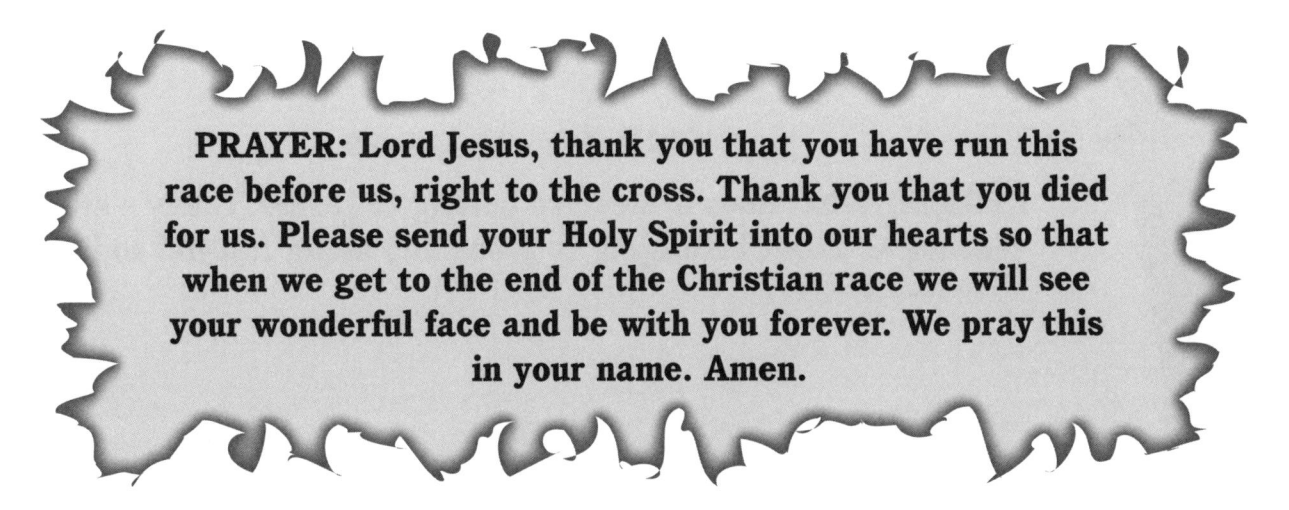

PRAYER: Lord Jesus, thank you that you have run this race before us, right to the cross. Thank you that you died for us. Please send your Holy Spirit into our hearts so that when we get to the end of the Christian race we will see your wonderful face and be with you forever. We pray this in your name. Amen.

BELONGING TO JESUS

Where do you Belong?

Have you ever been asked the question, 'Where do you belong?' You might reply, 'I belong to Glasgow,' or 'I live in Scotland.' Perhaps you come from another country like America or New Zealand. Someone might ask you 'Who do you belong to?' Would you say 'I belong to my mum and dad'? A married person would say, 'I belong to my husband' or 'I belong to my wife'.

READ: John 15: 18–19

LESSON: What does it mean to belong to Jesus? Today's story teaches us about belonging to Jesus and being faithful to him.

A New School

If you move to a new home or to a new school you might feel that you don't really belong. Things are different. Maybe someone will tell you, 'You don't belong here. You're not one of us! We're not going to play with you.' That can really hurt. Sometimes people don't like you when you belong to the Lord Jesus. Maybe they know that you go to Sunday school. They may even be nasty to you.

Listen to Jesus

Jesus says, 'Whenever that happens, remember that you belong to me. They do this to you because they don't love me either.'

Whenever this happens tell the Lord Jesus, 'Lord Jesus, this isn't my fault. It's because I belong to you.' Then he will say, 'I know it's because you belong to me. I know it's because you love me. And I know it's because you want to follow me that these things are happening. Trust me and I will take care of everything.'

Maybe one day some of the people who have been nasty to you will actually come to you and say, 'Can you help me to trust Jesus in the way you do?' So whenever you feel that because you belong to Jesus, you don't belong with your pals, remember this: Jesus is with you always. You always belong to him!

Let's pray that the Lord Jesus will help us to be faithful to him. Then through our lives, he will help others to trust him too.

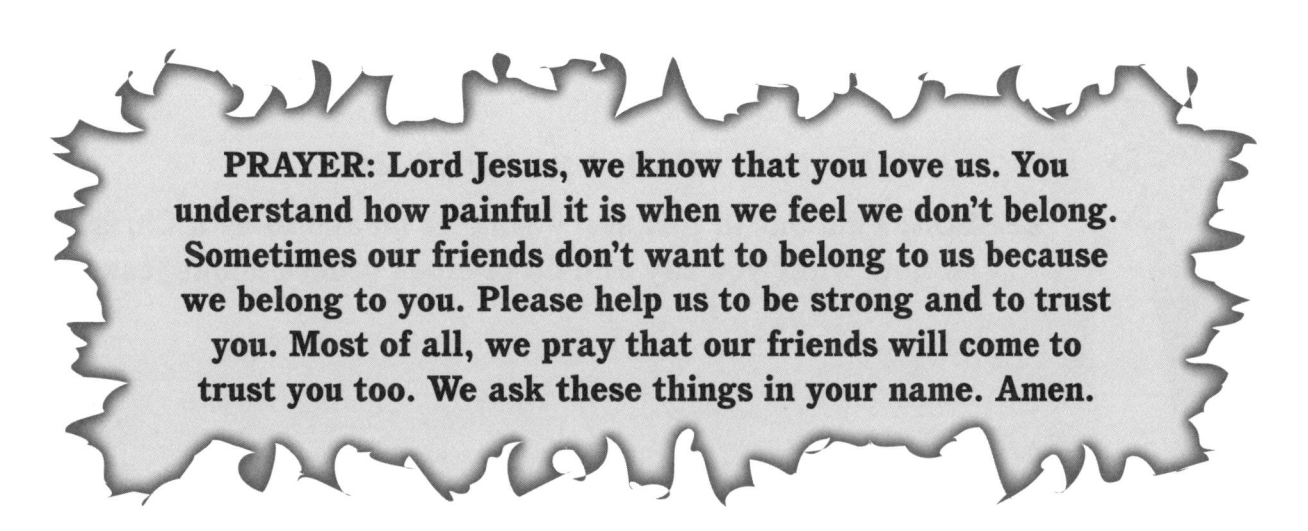

PRAYER: Lord Jesus, we know that you love us. You understand how painful it is when we feel we don't belong. Sometimes our friends don't want to belong to us because we belong to you. Please help us to be strong and to trust you. Most of all, we pray that our friends will come to trust you too. We ask these things in your name. Amen.

WHAT IS A CHRISTIAN?

The Making of a New Word

Acts 11:26 tells us, 'The disciples were first called Christians at Antioch'. That means that it was in the city of Antioch that somebody thought up a new word to describe the followers of Jesus. The new word they thought up was the word 'Christian' which means 'Christ's one'.

When I come across a word and I don't know what it means, I look it up in my dictionary. There are many different words in a dictionary – and each one of them has its own meaning.

You are Being Watched

Perhaps your friends at school or football club don't really know what the word 'Christian' means. How are they going to find out? They might not look up a dictionary. Perhaps your friends don't ever read the Bible. But they could find out, couldn't they? If you are a Christian they could find out what a Christian is like by looking at you!

If they watched the things that you said and did, they would be able to learn what it really means to be a Christian. Instead of having to read a dictionary, they could

READ: Acts 11: 19–26

LESSON: Find out in this story what it means to be a Christian and how what you say and do teaches others about Jesus.

come to you and say, 'How do I become a Christian like you?' Wouldn't that be amazing? That's exactly what happened in Antioch. The people in Antioch looked at the Christians and saw that they loved Jesus and that Jesus loved them. So they gave them the name 'Christ's Ones'. They knew that these people belonged to Jesus and followed him.

**PRAYER: Lord Jesus, we thank you that you speak to us through your Word in the Bible. By your Spirit, you are able to make us more and more like you. May our friends begin to see your love and your power in our lives and want to become Christians too. We pray this in your name.
Amen.**

NICKNAMES

Joseph's Nickname

Do you have a nickname? Do some of your friends have nicknames? In Acts 4: 36 a man called Joseph was given a nickname. He was a disciple of Jesus. Later on he became a close friend of the Apostle Paul. His real name was Joseph. He was originally from Cyprus, an island in the Mediterranean Sea, but he had moved to Jerusalem.

READ: Acts 4: 32–36

LESSON: Find out in this story about somebody's nickname and how we need to set our hearts on being like Jesus.

Joseph wasn't called 'Joseph' for long. The apostles gave him a nickname – 'Barnabas'. It means 'Son of Encouragement'. Barnabas was always helping and encouraging people. If you had come up to him and asked, 'What's your name?' he would have said, 'My name is Joseph Levi but my friends call me Barnabas.'

Do you Have a Nickname?

Are you ever called something different by your friends at school from what you're called at home? Michael at home – Mike at school, for example. Sometimes Mum and Dad don't like your name to be shortened. Perhaps you're called Jonny at school but Mum and Dad say, 'Jonathan' which is quite a mouthful.

Now I know what it's like to have a name that is a bit of a mouthful. My name is 'Sinclair B. Ferguson'. The B, stands for my middle name, 'Buchanan'. My mum gave me these names for two different reasons. One of the reasons was because she thought nobody would ever shorten or change the name 'Sinclair' into something else. (She was wrong!)

I'm sure Barnabas' mother called him 'Joseph' but maybe his pals at school called him 'Joe'. But when he became a Christian everybody called him 'Barnabas' because he was always helping them and encouraging them. That was why they called him 'Son of encouragement' – that's what 'Barnabas' means.

Choose a nickname for yourself from the list of words in Galatians 5:22-23. Then ask the Lord Jesus, 'Lord Jesus, make me like that nickname'. What name will you choose? Write this name down and say, 'Lord Jesus, help me to be like that so that I'll have a nickname that you alone know.' In Revelation, the last book of the Bible, it says that Jesus will give a nickname to every Christian that nobody else will know. What nickname would you like Jesus to give you?

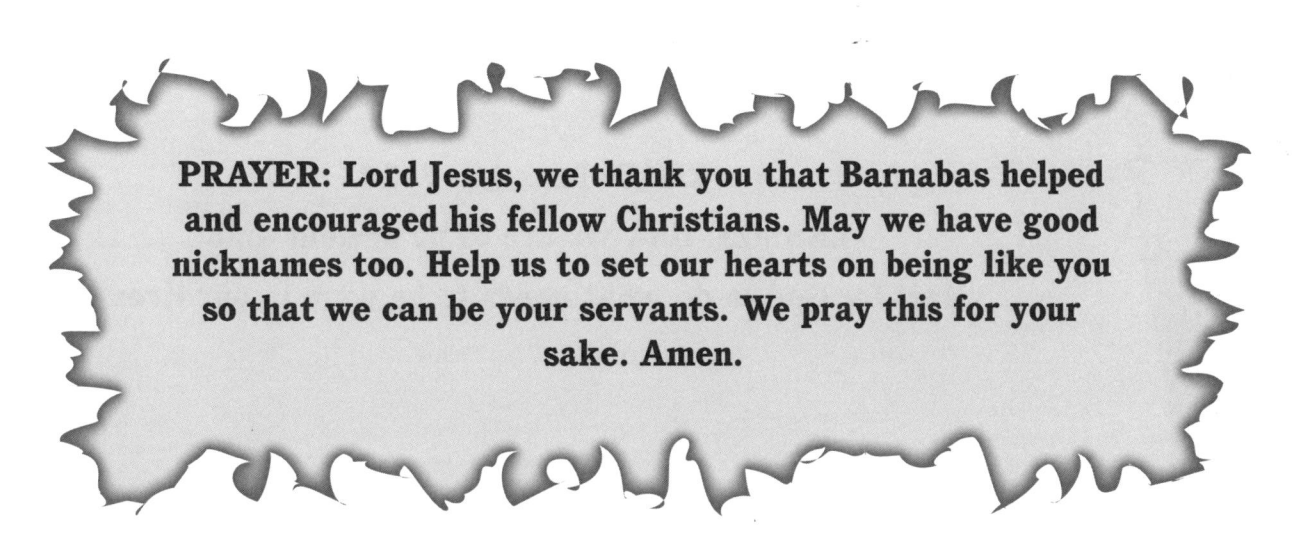

PRAYER: Lord Jesus, we thank you that Barnabas helped and encouraged his fellow Christians. May we have good nicknames too. Help us to set our hearts on being like you so that we can be your servants. We pray this for your sake. Amen.

HOW TO BE PATIENT

Learn from a Farmer

James 5: 7 says, 'Wait patiently for the Master's arrival.' What does it mean to wait patiently? Well, farmers have to do this all the time. They wait for their valuable crops to grow and ripen. They patiently let the rain do its slow but sure work. A farmer sows his seed, comes home, has his dinner, goes to bed, gets up in the morning, waits for the rain, goes to bed, goes to work in the morning, waits for the rain, day after day after day. Slowly harvest time comes. A farmer needs to be very patient. The Bible says that we are to be patient too. We are to wait patiently for the return of the Lord Jesus Christ.

READ: James 5: 7–12

LESSON: How we are to be patient and wait for God to do what needs to be done in our lives.

Be Patient

James uses two different words for being patient. The first word is MAKROTHUMEŌ. It is made up of two Greek words, THUMOS which means 'anger' and MAKROS which means 'long'. So the word makrothumeō is used when a person takes a long, long, long, long time to get irritated. In other words they are a patient person, like a farmer.

The farmer isn't sitting at his breakfast saying, 'I will make God hurry up with those rains.' He knows he must wait for God to send the rain so that there will be a harvest. While he waits he keeps working.

Wait Underneath

The other word James uses is HUPOMONĒ. This word means 'to remain or stay underneath'. What James was saying was that we are to 'wait', to 'wait underneath'.

Have you ever seen the Olympic weightlifters in the 'Snatch and Grab' competition? They pick up enormous weights and hold them above their heads. That's what this word HUPOMONĒ means. It means that when things are heavy or difficult, you're able to take the strain! To be a Christian, you need HUPOMONĒ. You need to know that God is producing a harvest of good things in your life. If you have HUPOMONĒ, even when things get bad and sore you are able to wait for God to produce the harvest.

If you are a Christian God is preparing a harvest for your life. He has plans for what he wants you to do. He'll maybe take you all over the world to serve the Lord Jesus. But first we must learn to trust him, and to wait.

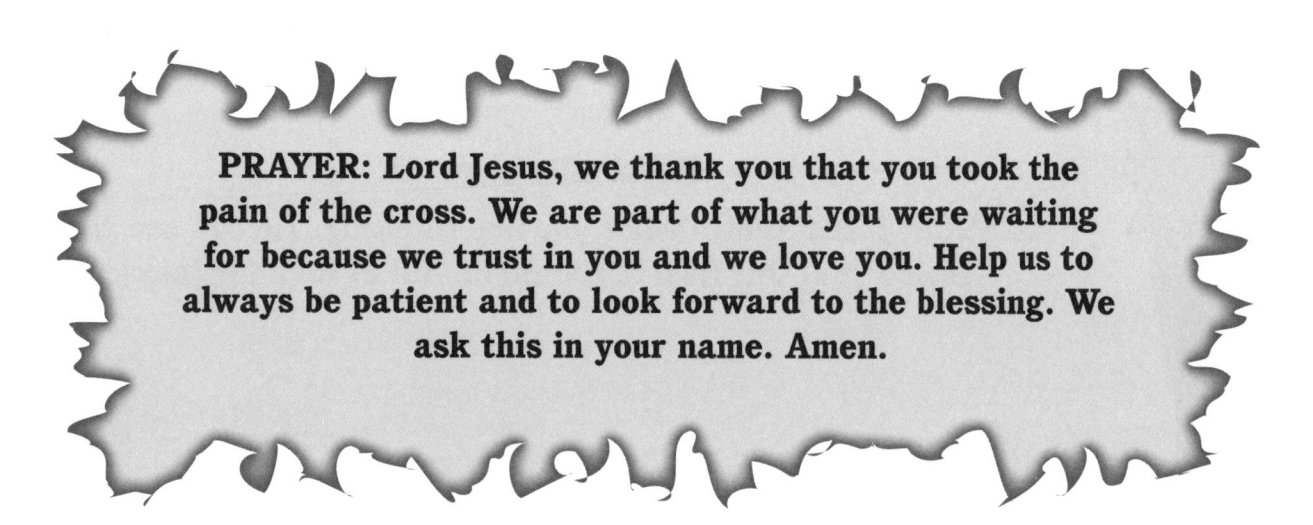

PRAYER: Lord Jesus, we thank you that you took the pain of the cross. We are part of what you were waiting for because we trust in you and we love you. Help us to always be patient and to look forward to the blessing. We ask this in your name. Amen.

THE HEART

Jesus Knows What's Inside

Matthew 23: 25 says, 'Jesus knows what's inside us.' I was once in a place called Seoul, Korea. One of my Korean friends said, 'Let's go to the Aquarium. I want you to see a very special fish.' Now, I'm not really interested in fish but my friend wanted me to see a very unusual fish. You could see all its bones! You could actually see right inside this fish. As I walked away I thought: 'What would we humans be like if we were like that fish? If other people could look right inside us they would see all the bits that are working – the heart pumping, the blood going round. They might even be able to see inside our stomach and find out what we'd had for breakfast!' No wonder we would keep wearing clothes!

But think of this. Jesus is able to see right inside you and see what you're thinking, and see what you're wanting.

How to See Inside Someone's Body

Have you ever seen an X-ray? It just looks like a piece of thin plastic, paper but when you hold it up to the light you can see pictures of inside your body. If a doctor takes an x-ray of a heart he can see a picture of that heart. Jesus sees right into that part of the heart where no one else can see. He can see right into the bit of you which loves God or doesn't love God.

I wonder if my heart is full of love for Jesus. That is what makes my heart work properly. Or is there something in my heart that's more important to me than Jesus? If there is, Jesus says, 'I'm going to have to fix that if you're going to be really well as a Christian'.

READ: Matthew 23

LESSON: Jesus knows what you are thinking. He can see right inside you. Our hearts should be full of love for Jesus.

We may say to Jesus, 'Don't do that, Jesus! I love that thing very much'. But he will say to us, 'If I don't fix it, it's going to do you a lot of damage. I can see right into your heart. I know if there is something there that we need to fix.' Then when Jesus does that, we say, 'Ah, I'm much healthier now!'

The way to live happily with the Lord Jesus is to listen to what he says and to obey his Word.

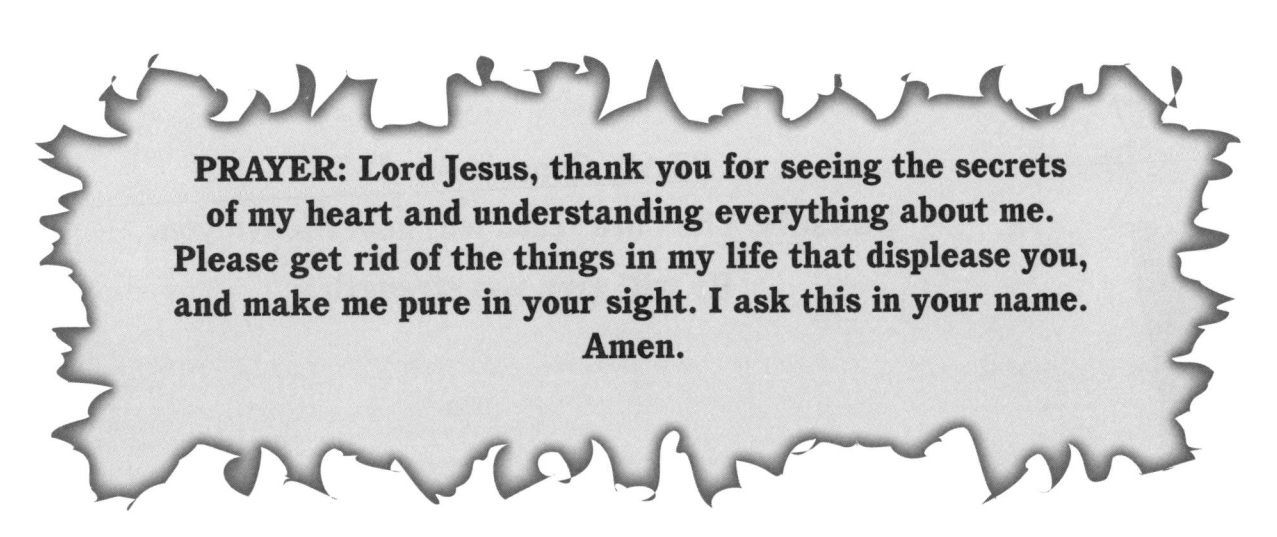

> **PRAYER:** Lord Jesus, thank you for seeing the secrets of my heart and understanding everything about me. Please get rid of the things in my life that displease you, and make me pure in your sight. I ask this in your name. Amen.

DON'T BE A COWARD

Coward

A coward is somebody who is afraid to do things they know they ought to.

Abraham was a wonderful man of faith. But sometimes he was brave and sometimes he was a coward.

He was brave when God said, 'I want you to leave your home and go to a new place, I am not going to tell you where this is. You will have to trust me.'

Abraham trusted God, got all his family together and they set off on their camels. At that point Abraham was very strong and brave. (This story is in Genesis 12.)

King Abimilech

However, sometimes Abraham was a coward. One time Abraham and his wife, Sarah, met King Abimilech. Sarah was very beautiful. Abraham was worried that if other men saw her they would steal her from him.

So when Abraham met King Abimilech he told him that Sarah was his sister and not his wife. What a coward! Just then all kinds of strange and really frightening things began to happen because Abraham had lied instead of being a courageous witness for God. (This part of Abraham's story is in Genesis 20.)

Are you a coward sometimes? When somebody says to you, 'Do you go to Sunday school? Do you follow the Lord Jesus?' we might feel a bit scared.

Instead of saying 'YES – I go to Sunday School, I love Sunday school, and YES - I

READ: Genesis 20: 1–5

LESSON: The Lord Jesus will never leave you.

He will give you strength.

follow the Lord Jesus', sometimes we get a bit wobbly inside and say, 'Well I have been at Sunday school. Oh yes, I have heard about Jesus.'

What are we going to do about our cowardly hearts? Well, we can say to the Lord Jesus 'Lord Jesus, I am just a jelly inside. I don't know what is going to happen to me if I tell my friends that I love you and I trust you.'

Jesus says, 'I will never, ever, ever, ever, leave you and I will be specially with you when you are scared. I will give you strength. Do not be afraid!'

Tell Jesus that you need his help. He has promised that he will never, ever, leave you and he will always be with you.

PRAYER: Lord Jesus, you knew what it was like to be afraid. We thank you that you conquered your fears and that you were faithful to your Father. We pray that you would help us to reach out to you, to trust in your promise, to live by your Word, and to be good witnesses to your grace. We pray this in your name, Amen.

JUST DO IT!

How to be a Christian

There were some people in the early church who said that to be a real Christian you needed to do the things that the Jewish people did. You had to observe the holy days and be careful about the things that you could eat and not eat. People like Paul said 'No. To be a Christian all we have to do is trust in the Lord Jesus, because he died to take away our sins.'

Remember Abraham

Some people said that they trusted in Jesus but they never showed it by being obedient. They didn't do the things that the Lord Jesus said. So James, Jesus' brother,

READ: James 2: 20–24

LESSON: If you are going to be a Christian you need to trust in the Lord Jesus. If we trust in Jesus we will want to do the things that Jesus tells us to do.

reminded them of Abraham who had trusted God and had obeyed him.

God had wanted Abraham to show how much he trusted him by doing something that was hard. He told Abraham to take his only son, Isaac, and offer him up as a sacrifice. Because Abraham trusted in God, he obeyed him. But just at the last minute God stopped Abraham and gave him a ram for the sacrifice instead. Abraham did not need to sacrifice his son. God did not want him to do that. He had shown that he trusted in the Lord. (You can read this story in Genesis 22.)

When James told this story he was trying to help the first Christians to understand that when we trust in Jesus, then we will do the things he says. We will help the people who are poor and needy. We will make friends with those who are lonely.

If we see people who are alone and don't befriend them then we are not really trusting in Jesus. If we don't show love and care for people who have no clothes then we aren't really following Jesus. We're not really being Christian.

If we trust in Jesus we will want to do the things that Jesus tells us to do. After all, Jesus is the Son of God. He actually became a sacrifice for our sins when he died on the cross. Because he has loved us like that, we can trust him and obey him.

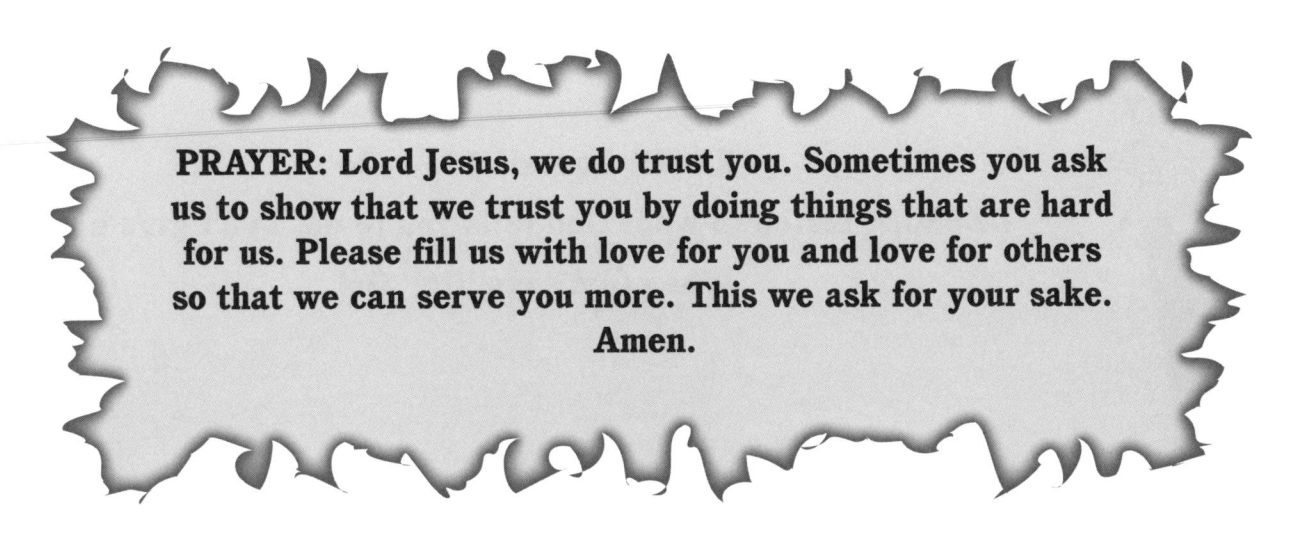

PRAYER: Lord Jesus, we do trust you. Sometimes you ask us to show that we trust you by doing things that are hard for us. Please fill us with love for you and love for others so that we can serve you more. This we ask for your sake.
Amen.

DON'T LOOK BACK

Lot's Choice

Abraham had a nephew called Lot. He was well named! Lot wanted 'a lot'! When Abraham gave him a choice of what land he would like he chose the best looking land. But the people who lived there were horrible and did horrible things. They didn't like God, and they didn't want to do what God said. The place was called Sodom. It was horrible.

Lot's Wife

God sent a terrible judgement on Sodom. The earth shook and hot sulphar rained down from the sky. But God sent two angels to rescue Lot and his family. God said 'You must not stop. You must not look back.' But Mrs. Lot did look back and she became a pillar of salt. All the sulphur rained down on top of her because she stopped.

I wonder why she looked back. Perhaps she wished that she hadn't left all her things behind. 'My jewels, my rings, that dolly I had when I was a little girl. Oh, they meant so much to me!'

What Jesus Said

Jesus said, 'Remember Lot's wife,' (Luke 17:22). When you decide to follow Jesus you can't look back. You've got to keep going. You can't give up.

READ: Genesis 19: 1–26

LESSON: Listen to what God tells you to do. Don't give up.

When God says 'Go!' Go!

Gladys Aylward

A young woman called Gladys Aylward believed God was calling her to go to China. She asked some Christians 'Will you send me to China?' She went from one group of Christians to another with the same question. Time after time she got the same answer. 'No, no! We can't send you to China.'

'But God has called me to go to China,' was Gladys' reply. 'If you're not going send me, I'll need to go to China on my own.' So that was what she did. She looked after little boys and girls who didn't have parents and she taught them about the Lord Jesus.

Gladys was faithful to the Lord Jesus. Some people had said to her 'It's too difficult to go.' But Gladys said, 'If God has told me to go, then I'm going.'

That's the way to live. When God tells you to go and you go, he blesses you. He keeps you and he guides you and he uses you. Gladys Aylward helped many people. Do you think you would be willing to go? It might just be to somebody in school or, it might be to faraway China. When God says, 'Go!' go.

(You can read the story of Gladys Aylward in *No Mountain Too High* by Myrna Grant.)

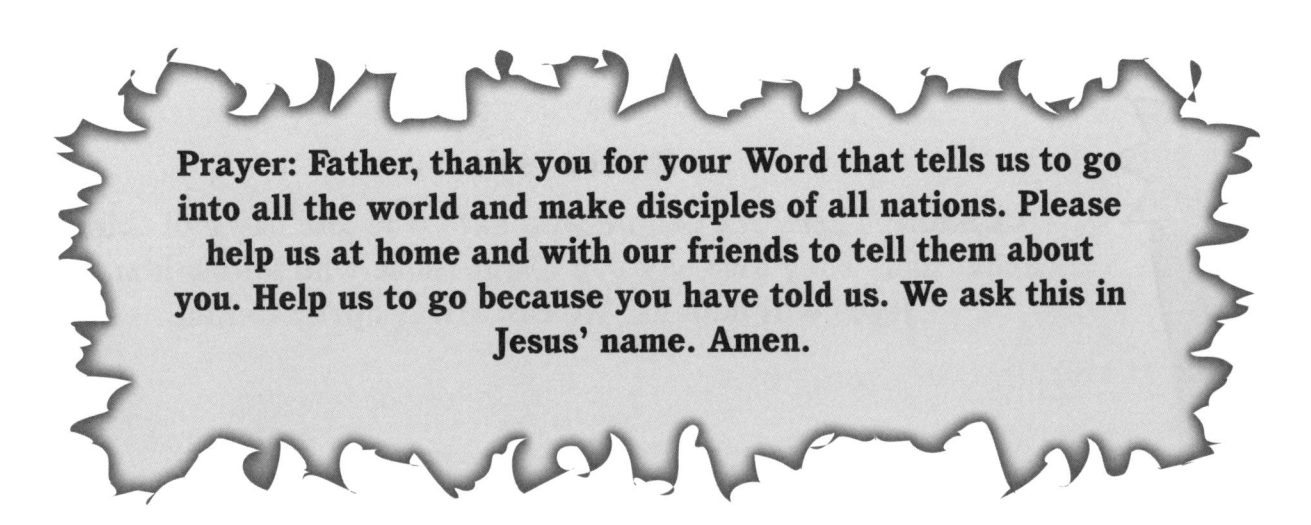

Prayer: Father, thank you for your Word that tells us to go into all the world and make disciples of all nations. Please help us at home and with our friends to tell them about you. Help us to go because you have told us. We ask this in Jesus' name. Amen.

A WICKED TONGUE

Trouble and Evil

Psalm 10 was written by a man who was not being treated very nicely. People were giving him a hard time. He said: 'Trouble and evil are under the wicked man's tongue'.

Sucking a Peppermint

Have you ever sucked a peppermint? What do you feel? Did you get the taste? It's strong. It's very strong! The taste is so strong that it's the only thing you can taste.

Psalm 10 is talking about people who have trouble and evil under their tongues. They say and do evil. Perhaps there is somebody like that in your school. They know that you love the Lord Jesus and want to follow him. Underneath their tongues are the words 'I hate Jesus.' What do you do when you meet somebody with these words under their tongue? What do you do when someone is horrible to you because you love Jesus and want to follow him? Here are some things you can do.

1. Speak to Jesus about it.
2. Remember the same things happened to Jesus. The reason it's happening to you is because you belong to Jesus and you love Jesus.
3. Remember Saul of Tarsus.

Saul of Tarsus? Why should we remember him?

READ: Psalm 10

LESSON: There are people who hate God and say evil things about him. They also say evil about those who follow him. But Jesus will help us. We can always pray to him.

Saul felt a deep-down hatred for the Lord Jesus. He especially hated Stephen because Stephen loved Jesus so much. But one day Saul himself became a Christian. Jesus stopped him on the road to Damascus and Saul became one of his disciples. (You can read about this in Acts 9.)

Being a Christian today can be really rough. Our world is full of people who have stuck peppermints of evil under their tongues. But Jesus is able to keep us and to help us.

PRAYER: Lord Jesus, you have called us to be very brave. Some people don't love you and are mean to us. Thank you for always being near to us. Bless us with courage. Help us to be faithful to you and to love you. Please help all our friends to trust in you and to become your disciples. In your great name we pray. Amen.

GROWING-UP

A Hard Question

Are you the oldest in the family, apart from Dad or Mum? I had a big brother. I was the younger son and he was the elder. Sometimes it's not easy having a big brother or sister. They're bigger and they're stronger. As well as that, they are almost always the first to do things. When I was quite little my big brother went to school before I did. I really wanted to go to school too because he was at school, but I had to wait.

My big brother always seemed to have more money than I had. And then he got to leave school before I did. He got a good job and he had lots more money and he had a car before I did. One day one of my teachers told me that I would never be like my big brother! So I used to wish that I could grow up quicker! I wanted to be able to skip a year or two. Why couldn't I just grow up?

Grow More Quickly

But there is absolutely nothing you can do to make yourself older, is there? You just cannot do it. You cannot make yourself grow up more quickly. You've got to take one day at a time.

However, you can grow up more quickly as a Christian. Luke 2: 52 says that Jesus grew up quickly. He became wise and he loved God very much.

READ: Luke 2: 41–52

LESSON: With God's help you can grow up as a Christian. It doesn't matter how old you are.

How can I do that too? Here are three things that will help you to do this.

1. Get to know your Bible. Read it or ask someone to read it to you.

2. Speak to God in prayer and get to know him that way.

3. Serve him. Tell others about him. Love him. Do the things that he wants you to do and trust him absolutely.

Will you think about these three things? There are things that will really help you to grow and grow. You might grow so much that you'll be taller as a Christian than somebody who is much taller in height than you are.

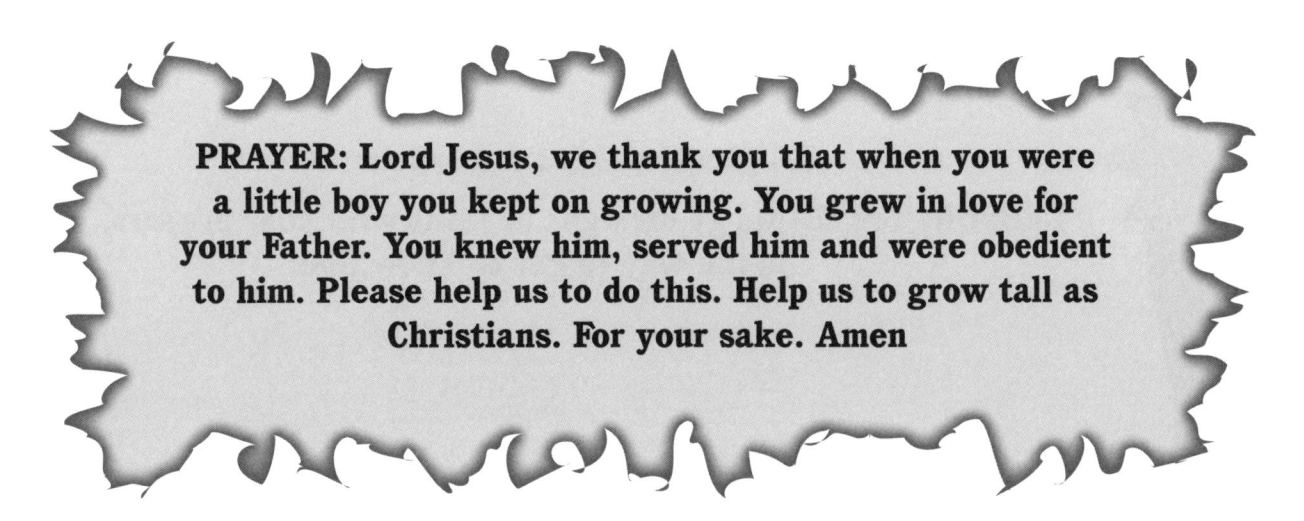

PRAYER: Lord Jesus, we thank you that when you were a little boy you kept on growing. You grew in love for your Father. You knew him, served him and were obedient to him. Please help us to do this. Help us to grow tall as Christians. For your sake. Amen

FOLLOW THE WAY

How to Get to Know God

When Paul spoke about being a follower of the Way, he was speaking about being a follower of Jesus, because Jesus is the Way to get to know God.

One day I was reading the local newspaper when I saw an advert that caught my eye. It said, 'Ask Saint Jude for three favours'. What does that mean? I think it means that you're supposed to ask St Jude for something special to happen. Perhaps you've heard of people who say special prayers to Mary for nine days. A 'novena' is a prayer that some people say for nine days in succession.

Don't you think it is a big mistake to pray to Mary or Jude when our Father God wants us to pray to him? Jesus says, 'Pray in my name. I am the Way to the Father.'

READ: Acts 24: 10–16; John 14: 6

LESSON: You should go straight to Jesus with your prayers. Jesus is the way to get to know God.

The Way is Jesus

Perhaps these people think that Jesus is too busy? Maybe they think to themselves, 'I'm afraid of Jesus, I'd better go to somebody else.'

The world is full of people who don't know the Way. Paul said he was a follower of the Way, the one and only Way to get to God. And who is the Way? The Way to God is the Lord Jesus Christ.

If we know the Way we should tell others about him! Tell somebody who doesn't know Jesus that he is the Way to God.

If we're following Jesus, loving Jesus, serving Jesus, trusting Jesus, we will want to get to know Jesus better! But lots of your friends don't know the Way. They're lost! Let's pray to the Lord Jesus and say, 'Help me to tell my friends about you.' Jesus will answer that prayer.

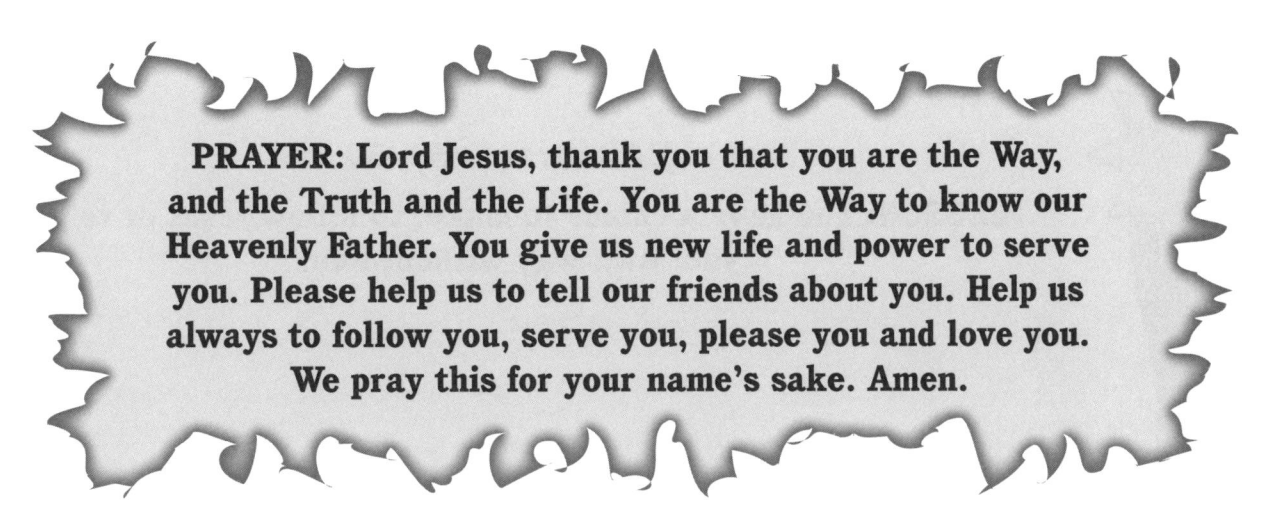

> **PRAYER:** Lord Jesus, thank you that you are the Way, and the Truth and the Life. You are the Way to know our Heavenly Father. You give us new life and power to serve you. Please help us to tell our friends about you. Help us always to follow you, serve you, please you and love you. We pray this for your name's sake. Amen.

Paul Casts His Vote

Voting in an Election

Do you know what age you need to be to vote? You have to be eighteen to vote for a member of Parliament in the United Kingdom and United States of America.

A Vote for Life

In Acts, Chapter 7, we are told that Paul cast his vote against the Christians. He said, 'I don't want the Christians.' This was before he believed in Jesus Christ of course. People knew him then as Saul of Tarsus. When he was asked, 'Will we let this Christian called Stephen live?' Paul said, 'Let's stone him!' They did. The men had to take their coats off to do it and they said to Saul, 'You watch my coat.' Paul didn't mind doing that. He hated Christians.

READ: Acts 7: 54–59

LESSON: You have a choice to make: to follow Jesus or to go your own way without him.

But someone else had a vote. When Saul went off to find more Christians to stone to death, Jesus had already decided on his vote. Saul was murdering all these Christians who trusted in Jesus and followed him. How do you think Jesus had voted? Did he say 'Saul must die' or did he say 'Let him live'? When Jesus had voted, he voted 'Live!'

Saul was on the way to Damascus when Jesus met him. A bright light blinded him. Saul said, 'Lord, who are you?' Jesus showed Saul mercy and Saul came to know Jesus Christ as his Lord and Saviour. Even though Saul had voted against Jesus and his followers, Jesus had already voted for Saul. He had died for Saul. He forgave him and brought him into the family of God.

We have got to vote about something too. We've got to vote about Jesus. What will your vote be? Will it be 'No, I don't want you, Jesus'? Or will it be 'Yes! I want to trust Jesus and to love Jesus and to live for Jesus'?

Thankfully you don't need to be eighteen to vote about this. You can trust in Jesus at any age. You can tell Jesus you love him at any time. 'Yes, Jesus. I trust you and love you and want to serve you.'

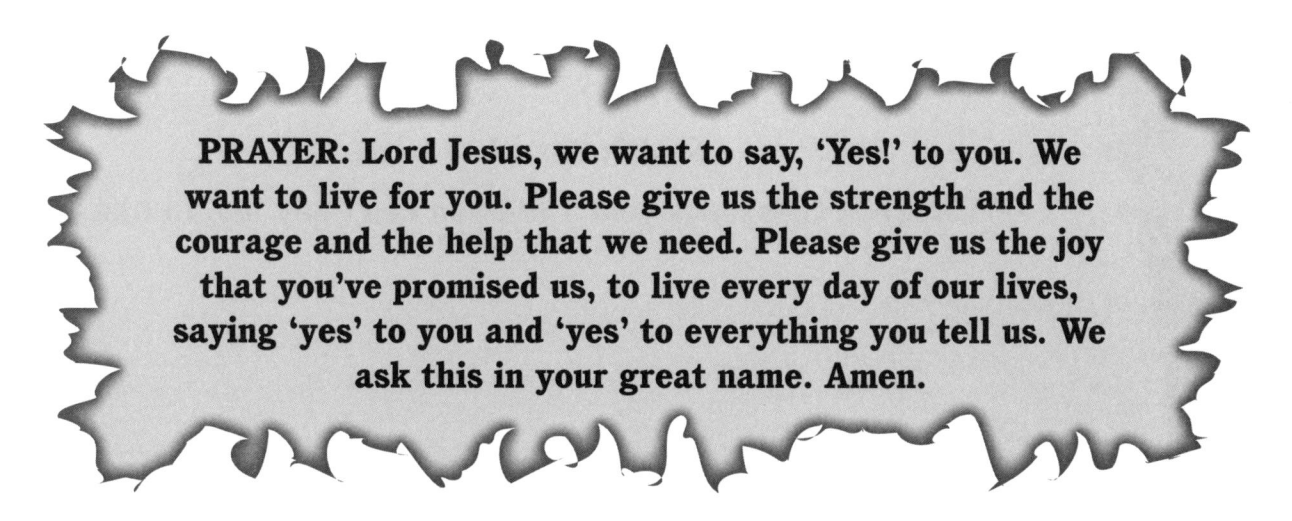

PRAYER: Lord Jesus, we want to say, 'Yes!' to you. We want to live for you. Please give us the strength and the courage and the help that we need. Please give us the joy that you've promised us, to live every day of our lives, saying 'yes' to you and 'yes' to everything you tell us. We ask this in your great name. Amen.

OXY - WHAT?

Words That Don't Make Sense!

What would you think of someone who came up to you and said 'Hurry up now! Slowly!'? It doesn't really make sense does it? It's saying two words that mean opposite things. 'Hurry' and 'Slow'! We call that an OXYMORON.

Do you know what a 'moron' is? It means somebody who is really stupid. 'Oxy' comes from a Greek word that means sharp. If someone describes you as being 'sharp' they usually mean you are clever. They are certainly not describing you as being stupid. So 'Oxy', which means sharp and 'Moron', which means stupid don't really go together. Just like 'Hurry up - slowly.'

So an oxymoron is when you put two words together that don't really belong.

READ: Acts 11: 1–18

LESSON: If Jesus is your Lord you can't say 'no' to him.

Two words that don't belong together

Peter used an oxymoron in Acts 11: 8. He said: 'Surely not, Lord!' Do you see two words in this sentence that don't belong together? 'Not' and 'Lord.' That's like saying, 'No, Lord.' These words just don't go together.

Peter should have known not to use these words. It wasn't the first time that he had said them. He told Jesus more than once, 'No, Lord!'

If somebody is your Lord, you don't ever say 'no' to them. The words that belong together are 'Yes, Lord'. If you read Acts, Chapter 11, you will find out why Peter was saying 'No' and what happened when he realised that this was wrong.

I wonder if you are saying 'No' to the Lord Jesus today? What are you saying 'No' about?

Remember that the words 'Lord' and 'No' are an oxymoron. Jesus doesn't want any oxymorons in your life!

PRAYER: Lord Jesus, we thank you that you have done everything for us. You never said 'No, Lord' to your Heavenly Father. Because we belong to you, we want to be like you. We pray that you would help us every day to say 'Yes, Lord Jesus – anything you want, I will do.' We pray this in your name. Amen.

NICODEMUS

How Many Birthdays?

You only have one birthday every year. However, there's somebody in the United Kingdom who has two. The British Monarch has an official birthday and an actual birthday. But you and I have only got one birthday.

Do you remember anything about the day you were born? Can you remember what happened? Of course you don't. You might have been told about it, or even seen photographs, but you won't remember the day at all.

Nicodemus Visits Jesus

One night a man called Nicodemus came to see Jesus. He wanted to find out about belonging to the kingdom of God. He wanted to speak to Jesus about being part of God's family.

Jesus said to him, 'Nicodemus, you'll never be part of God's family until you've had two birthdays.'

Now Nicodemus couldn't work this out. He said to Jesus, 'But I'm quite an old man. I can't get younger and smaller and shrink right back to the beginning again so that I can have another birthday! How can I possibly have two birthdays? Why do I need to have two birthdays if I'm going to be in God's family?'

Jesus said to him, 'Nicodemus, you need to have two birthdays. You had one birthday when you were born into your own family. But if you're going to be born into God's family, you'll need to have another birthday.'

Nicodemus said, 'I don't think I understand that, Jesus.'

READ: John 3: 1–21

LESSON: To belong to the family of God the Holy Spirit needs to work in your heart. You need to be born again.

So Jesus explained it to him. 'This second birthday can be yours when the Holy Spirit works in your heart and you are born again.'

When babies are born, how do you know that the baby is alive? Babies cry – and that's how you know that they're alive. Babies usually cry when they want to be fed which is another sign that the baby is alive. The baby is beginning to grow and needs to have food. That's why babies cry – loudly!

Being born again is a bit like that. The first sign that you've been born again is that you cry out to God and you call him 'Father'. When we call God 'Father, Dear Father' – that's one of the signs that the Holy Spirit has worked in our hearts and we belong to his family.

Jesus said, 'When you call my Father, "Heavenly Father" and you love him and trust him, that's the sign that the Spirit has given you another birthday.'

So, although you have one birthday it is possible for you to have two. If you love and trust in Jesus then you will have had a second birthday. Maybe, like your own birthday, you can't remember anything about it. But if you trust in the Lord Jesus Christ the Holy Spirit has begun to work in your heart. When you are asked when your birthday is, you can say, 'Well, I've got the birthday when I came into the world. And because I love the Lord Jesus, and trust the Heavenly Father, I have had another birthday.'

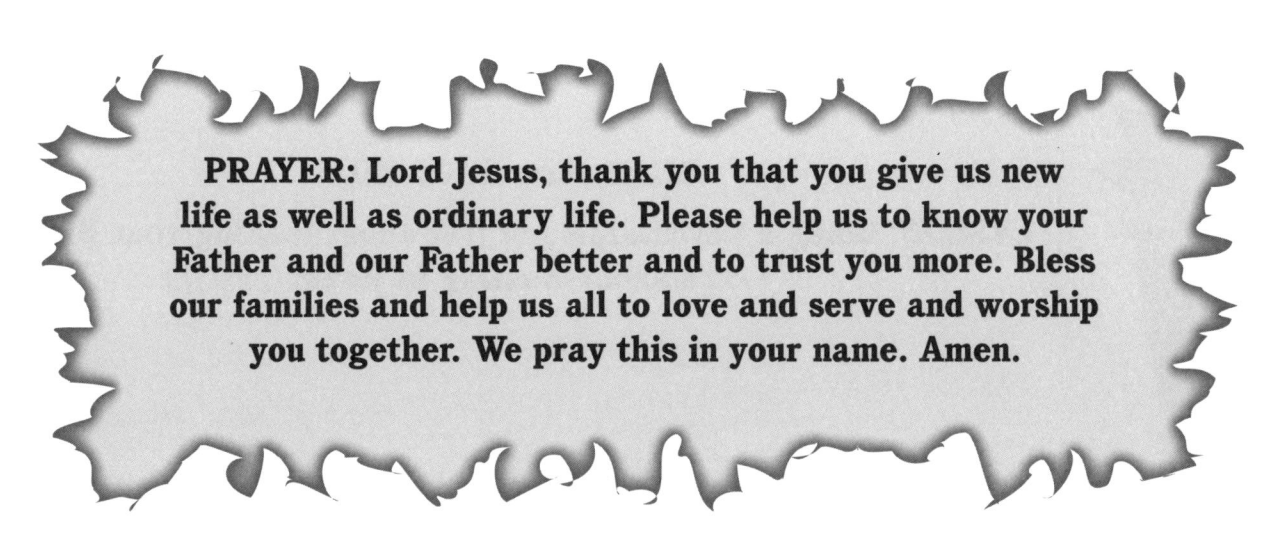

PRAYER: Lord Jesus, thank you that you give us new life as well as ordinary life. Please help us to know your Father and our Father better and to trust you more. Bless our families and help us all to love and serve and worship you together. We pray this in your name. Amen.

AN ETHIOPIAN VISITOR

Philip Leaves for the Desert

When Jesus went back into heaven he sent the Holy Spirit to the church. Christians then started going to all kinds of different places, telling people about Jesus.

A man called Philip went to Samaria where many people became Christians. But then God did a strange thing. Instead of keeping Philip in a place where so many people were becoming Christians – he sent him to a place where there was nobody! Well, almost nobody.

Philip was sent to the Gaza desert. There he saw a chariot belonging to a man from the country of Ethiopia. The man was reading something out loud. He was reading from Isaiah, Chapter 53, about a man who was taken like a lamb to be killed and was like a sheep and didn't say anything.

READ: Acts 8: 26–40

LESSON: Being a Christian is not just about reading your Bible – it's about trusting in Jesus.

The Holy Spirit told Philip to catch up with the chariot. So he ran up alongside it and called over to the Ethiopian, 'Do you understand what that is all about?' The Ethiopian looked at him and said, 'No I don't. I need someone to explain it to me.' So he invited Philip to come up and sit beside him in the chariot.

This Ethiopian man had been to Jerusalem to worship God. He even had his own copy of the Book of Isaiah. However, he still didn't know the Lord Jesus. So Philip sat down beside him and said, 'I need to tell you something. It's not just reading your Bible that's important. It's knowing and trusting Jesus. Isaiah is talking here about Jesus.' Philip told him all about Jesus, and the man from Ethiopia became a Christian.'

What Does it Mean to be a Christian?

When I was your age I read my Bible day after day and I thought that that's what it meant to be a Christian. I thought that to be a Christian you had to read your Bible, say a prayer and sometimes help an old lady across the road. Although I was reading my Bible, I still didn't know Jesus or trust in him. Then I read John, Chapter 5, verses 39–40. As I read them, it was if a light had been turned on! Jesus said this: 'You are searching the Scriptures and you think that you will find life in them but you're still not coming to trust in me in order to have real life.'

That was what I was missing. I hadn't really been trusting in Jesus at all.

Now here's a question for you. We read the Bible in church. We read the Bible in Sunday school. Maybe we also read the Bible at home. But are we trusting the Lord Jesus? Are we living for him?

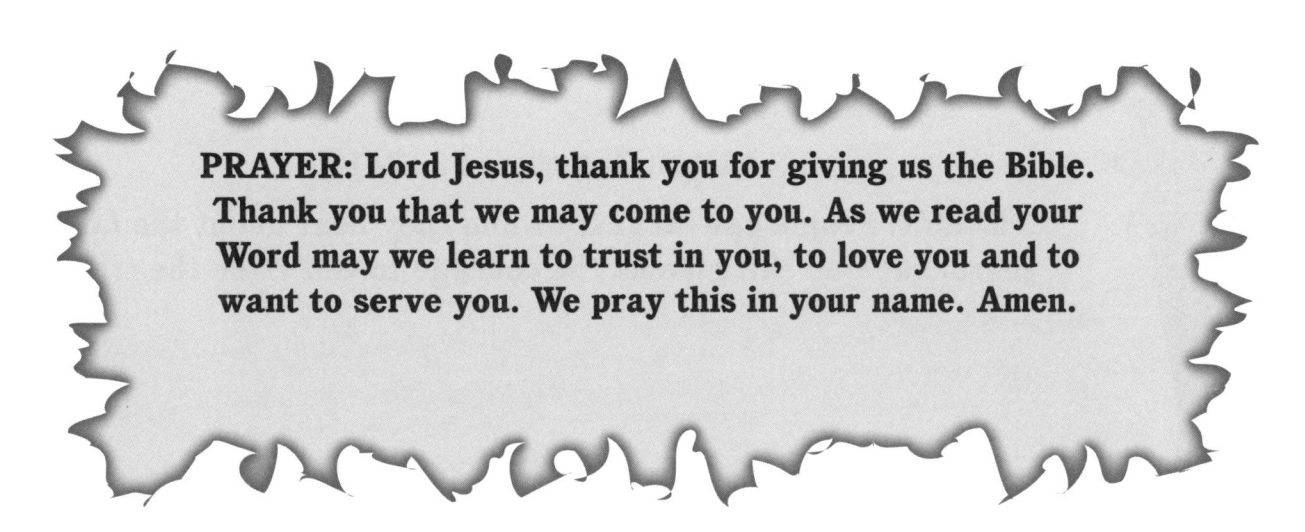

> **PRAYER: Lord Jesus, thank you for giving us the Bible. Thank you that we may come to you. As we read your Word may we learn to trust in you, to love you and to want to serve you. We pray this in your name. Amen.**

GET IN A TIME MACHINE

Go Back in Time to Antioch

I want you to imagine that you can get into a great big time machine. You are going to go back in time to the year 100 and still keep travelling until you stop somewhere about the year 50. Imagine you're at the church that Paul was a member of in Antioch. They are just about to have a church picnic.

Antioch is near the Mediterranean Sea where it's nice and warm. Because all the children are playing they are feeling quite hot and sweaty. Some of the adults are also feeling the heat. Most of the men have rolled up their sleeves. Do you notice that the Apostle Paul has done the same? What's that you see on his arms? They

READ: Galatians 6: 12–18

LESSON: People can be nasty when they hear about the Lord Jesus, but God can give us the courage to tell them the truth.

look like bruises. And look at his legs - they have cuts all over them. You turn and say to someone, 'What happened to him?'

An older boy whispers to you, 'The Apostle Paul was telling people about Jesus and some of them attacked him. They threw great big stones at him. He was almost killed'.

Later on in the afternoon you sit down near Paul. He is finishing writing a letter. Just at the end he writes down these words, 'I have on my body the marks of the Lord Jesus.' (You can read these words in Galatians 6:17). You realise that Paul is willing to die for the Lord Jesus. You want to ask him all kinds of questions. Oh dear, it's time for you to leave Bible times and come back to the 21st century!

Be Faithful and Brave

Before Paul became a Christian he was known as Saul of Tarsus. But can you remember the name of the man who was ready to die for the Lord Jesus in order that Saul of Tarsus might become a Christian? His name was Stephen. When he was being stoned to death Saul actually looked after the coats of the people who were throwing the stones.

As he looked on perhaps Saul thought, 'That man must really love Jesus if he's willing to die for him. I wonder if what he said about Jesus is really true?'

Later, on the road to Damascus, Saul discovered for himself that it was true. Stephen had been prepared to die so that Saul would become a Christian. Years later after Saul had changed his name to Paul he too was prepared to die so that others would come to know Jesus Christ as their Lord and Saviour.

I don't suppose that people will often throw things at you because you're a Christian. But sometimes people may be nasty. Remember this: sometimes the people who are mad at you for loving Jesus are the very people that God is going to change. So be faithful and be brave. Your enemies may one day become friends of Jesus.

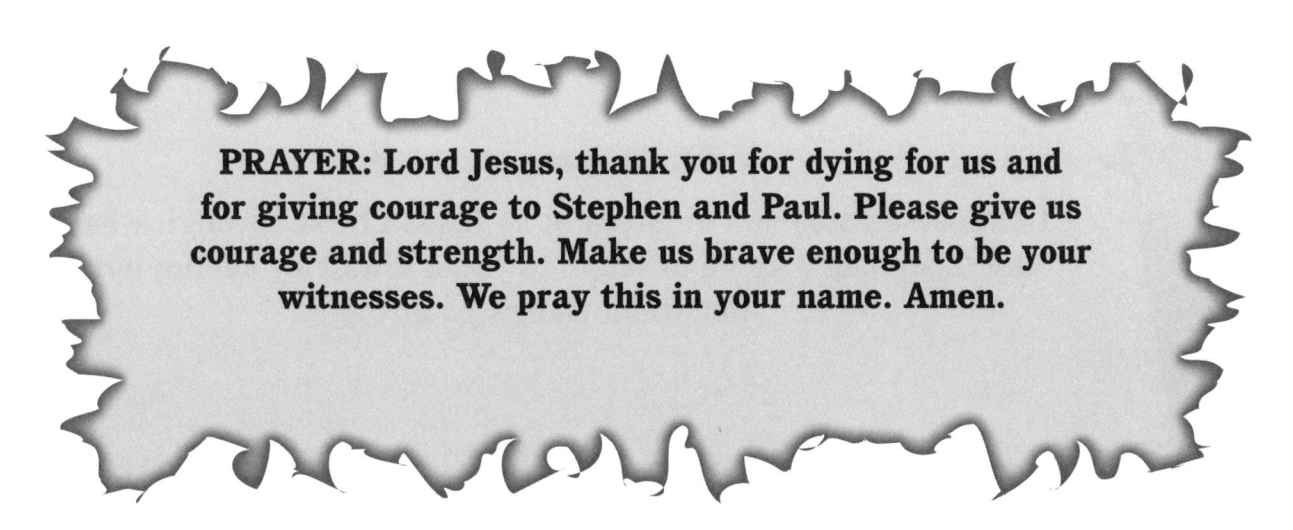

PRAYER: Lord Jesus, thank you for dying for us and for giving courage to Stephen and Paul. Please give us courage and strength. Make us brave enough to be your witnesses. We pray this in your name. Amen.

PAUL IN TROUBLE

In Philippi

Paul always seemed to get into trouble. Often when he preached about Jesus somebody got angry with him or beat him up or tried to stone him to death.

When Paul came to Philippi he told the people there about the Lord Jesus. Some were delighted. They had never heard about Jesus before. They came to trust in Jesus as their Saviour. But wherever Paul went there were always some people who wanted to stop him speaking about Jesus. This is what happened in Philippi.

READ: Acts 16: 16–40

LESSON: People can be brought to Jesus Christ through what we say. They can also be brought to Jesus Christ by seeing how we act when things go wrong.

However, this time his friend, Silas, was with him. The two men were thrown into the jail and had their legs fastened in the stocks so that they wouldn't escape. That must have been horrible for them! But even all these horrible things didn't stop them from singing hymns to God. They were still singing hymns at midnight when an earthquake struck.

The jailor was terrified . He rushed up to Paul and asked 'What must I do to be saved by Jesus?'

Paul and Silas told him to trust in Jesus. That night the jailor became a Christian.

What's the Important Thing?

Sometimes people are brought to trust in the Lord Jesus by what we say about him. However, they can also be brought to Jesus by watching us and seeing what we do when things go wrong.

Everything seemed to be going wrong for Paul and Silas. But when they were stuck in the stocks what did they do? They turned to each other and they said, 'Let's praise Jesus because he's such a wonderful Saviour.'

When the earthquake began, Paul and Silas were sore, beaten, lonely men in a horrid prison. But they still sang praises about Jesus. When the jailor saw that perhaps he thought, 'What an amazing Saviour this Jesus must be!'

How is it possible to sing God's praises when things are going wrong? The only way you can do it is if the Lord Jesus is living in your life. When things begin to go wrong, you can still praise him. Then your friends will say, 'Why is it that she praises Jesus all the time?' Maybe they'll be like that Philippian jailor and they'll ask you how to be saved by Jesus.

Let's pray that, like Paul and Silas, we'll be able to praise the Lord Jesus so that others will get to know him through us.

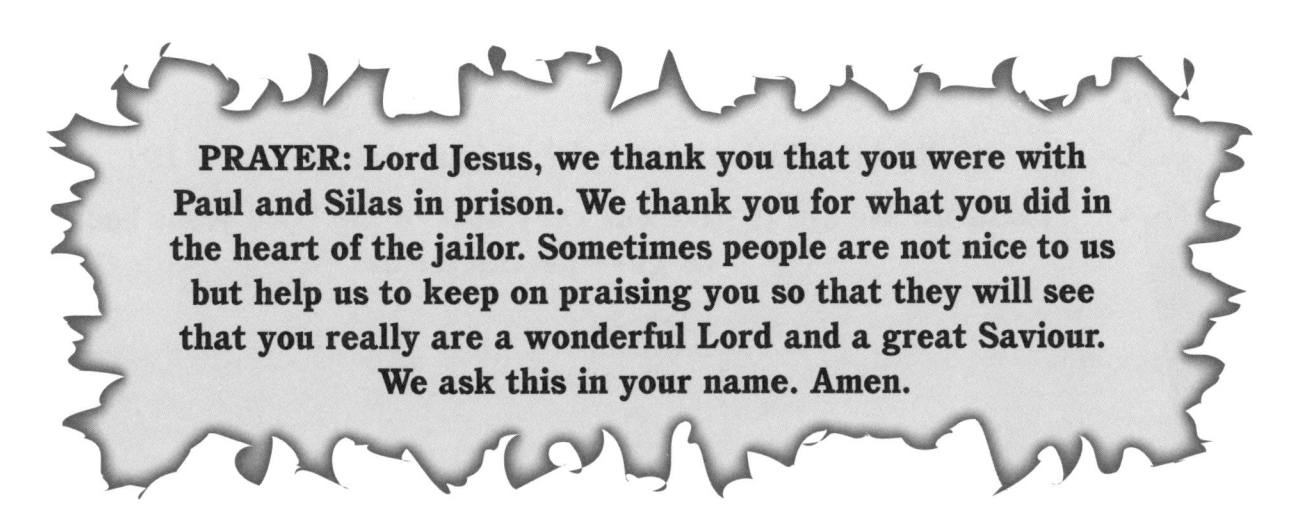

PRAYER: Lord Jesus, we thank you that you were with Paul and Silas in prison. We thank you for what you did in the heart of the jailor. Sometimes people are not nice to us but help us to keep on praising you so that they will see that you really are a wonderful Lord and a great Saviour. We ask this in your name. Amen.

DAVID'S BIG THREE

The Cave of Adullum

In Philippians 2:17 Paul wrote about his life being a 'drink offering'. What is a drink offering and what does it mean to make your life a 'drink offering'? King David was once forced to live in a cave. People were trying to kill him. So David and some of his friends went to hide in the Cave of Adullum.

Can you imagine what it would have been like living in that cave? They wouldn't have had any electricity or lights. They might have had some smoky old lamps. They certainly wouldn't have had a fridge or freezer. There were no shops or supermarkets near by. And with all the men who were hiding with David it must have been smelly and stuffy in that cave!

But the strangest thing of all would have been the people living with David in the cave. Some of David's followers were wild men, strong and fierce. Three of these men were particularly brave. Let's call them 'The Big Three'. They were special friends of David and very loyal to him.

One day David was sitting in the cave. He remembered the well in the little town of Bethlehem where he was born. He remembered how sweet and fresh the water was there. He said out loud, 'Ah, I'd give anything for a drink of water from the well in Bethlehem!'

The Big Three loved David so much that they said to each other, 'Let's go and get him some of that water!'

Now Bethlehem was surrounded by their enemies, the Philistines. Any normal soldier would never have made it to the well. But the Big Three managed it!

READ: Philippians 2: 17; 1 Chronicles 11: 15–19.

LESSON: We are to give our very best to the Lord Jesus because he gave his life for us.

One night they made their way past the Philistines and brought back to David a bottle of Bethlehem water. They ran back into the cave shouting, 'David! David! Look what we've got! Look what we've got!'

David thought, 'I can't drink this. These men have risked their lives just to get me a drink of water from Bethlehem. The only thing I can do is give this water to the Lord.'

So David prayed to God and said, 'Lord, this is the very best I've got and I want you to have it.' Can you believe that he poured the water out?

That's what Paul meant when he spoke about his life being a drink offering. He wanted to give his best to the Lord Jesus. Why? Because Jesus poured out his life as a drink offering to save us.

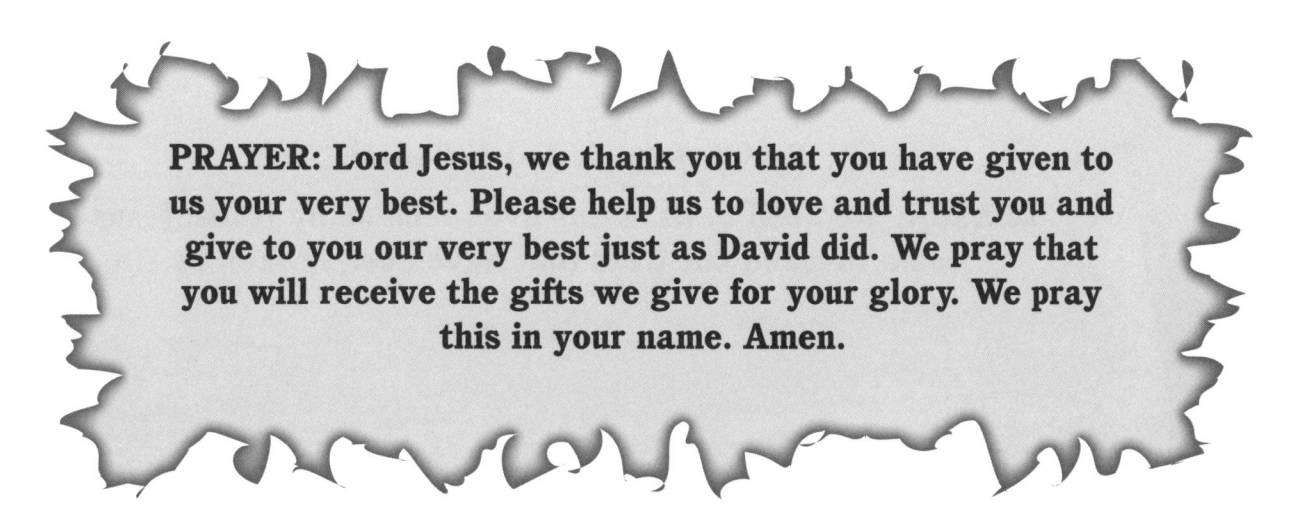

PRAYER: Lord Jesus, we thank you that you have given to us your very best. Please help us to love and trust you and give to you our very best just as David did. We pray that you will receive the gifts we give for your glory. We pray this in your name. Amen.

A MAN BORN BLIND

How does a Blind Person Read?

When people lose their sight sometimes they learn to use their other senses better than they did before. These senses often become stronger to make up for the sense that they don't have. How do blind people read when they can't see the letters? They use Braille. They use their fingers to feel little raised up dots on the page. Somehow or other people who have no sight develop tremendous powers of touching as well as hearing.

One day Jesus met a man who had been blind from birth. He couldn't see a thing. He heard Jesus getting down on his knees. Jesus picked up some dirt and spat on it. He made the dirt into a kind of paste and then told the blind man to 'Hold still'.

READ: John 9: 1–12; Genesis 2: 7

LESSON: We need to have our lives remade by Jesus. Jesus has come to mend our lives that have been broken by sin.

He dabbed the paste all over the man's eyes. Then he said 'Go to the pool of Siloam. Wash your eyes and then you'll be able to see'.

The man did as he was told and went to the pool of Siloam. He washed his eyes. Then for the first time in his life, he could see!

Now Jesus could have made that blind man see just by saying 'You can see now, go home.' So why did he go to all the bother of making a paste and dabbing it on the man's eyes?

Right at the beginning the Bible tells us how God made human beings out of mud. I think Jesus used the mud to teach the blind man (and to teach us) that we need to be remade. We need to be made new. That was why Jesus came into the world. He came to make people new.

Isn't that wonderful? Jesus has come into the world to pick up the pieces of our lives that have been broken by our sin and by other people's sin. If you are ever walking in the mud, remember what Jesus could do with mud!

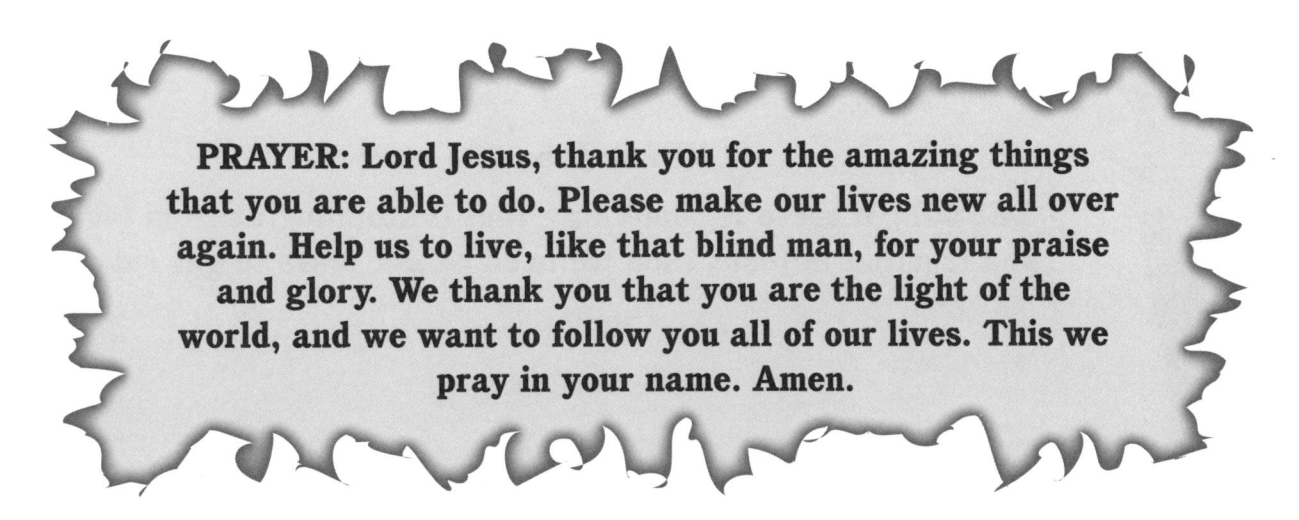

PRAYER: Lord Jesus, thank you for the amazing things that you are able to do. Please make our lives new all over again. Help us to live, like that blind man, for your praise and glory. We thank you that you are the light of the world, and we want to follow you all of our lives. This we pray in your name. Amen.

JUDAS

The Betrayer

Just before Jesus died his disciples were with him in a little room. They were going to celebrate the Jewish Passover. However, the disciples were too proud to wash each other's dirty feet. Who do you think washed them instead? Yes, Jesus did. Then Jesus sat down at the table and said, 'One of you is going to let me down and betray me.'

Who betrayed Jesus? It was Judas. He betrayed Jesus for the same amount of money that it would have cost to buy a slave.

How could somebody who had been with Jesus for three years possibly betray him?

Get out the Tweezers

Sometimes when you fall you can get a bit of grit or a slither of wood in your hand. Has that ever happened to you? Your mum might then go to the First Aid Box and get out the tweezers. She might not get it all out. What does she do then? Does she go to her sewing box and get out a pin? Then she sterilises the pin in boiling water. She uses that pin to try to get the grit out. It's important to get things like that out of your hand. If you don't get the dirt out, your hand might swell up and it could be poisoned.

Judas Betrays Jesus

Something like this happened in Judas' heart. For quite a long time Jesus had been saying to him 'Judas, there's something I need to get out of your life.' He'd been

READ: John 13: 1–30

LESSON: If there is something that is stopping us from loving and trusting in Jesus then we need to ask Jesus to get rid of it.

giving him little hints and using his loving tweezers to try to get the dirt out of Judas' heart. Jesus even washed Judas' feet. But he knew that Judas did not want Jesus to wash his heart. Jesus knew that Judas was going to betray him. And that is exactly what Judas did.

Judas' Heart

How could Judas possibly betray Jesus? Well, there was something in Judas' heart that he wouldn't let Jesus take away.

When I think about that, I ask myself, 'Is there something in my heart that I won't give up to Jesus?' If there is, I need to say, 'Lord Jesus, just take it out of my heart, because I want to love you with all my heart.' I need to say this. And you need to say it too. If you do this you'll live the rest of your life, loving and serving him and you'll never, ever, ever become like Judas and betray Jesus.

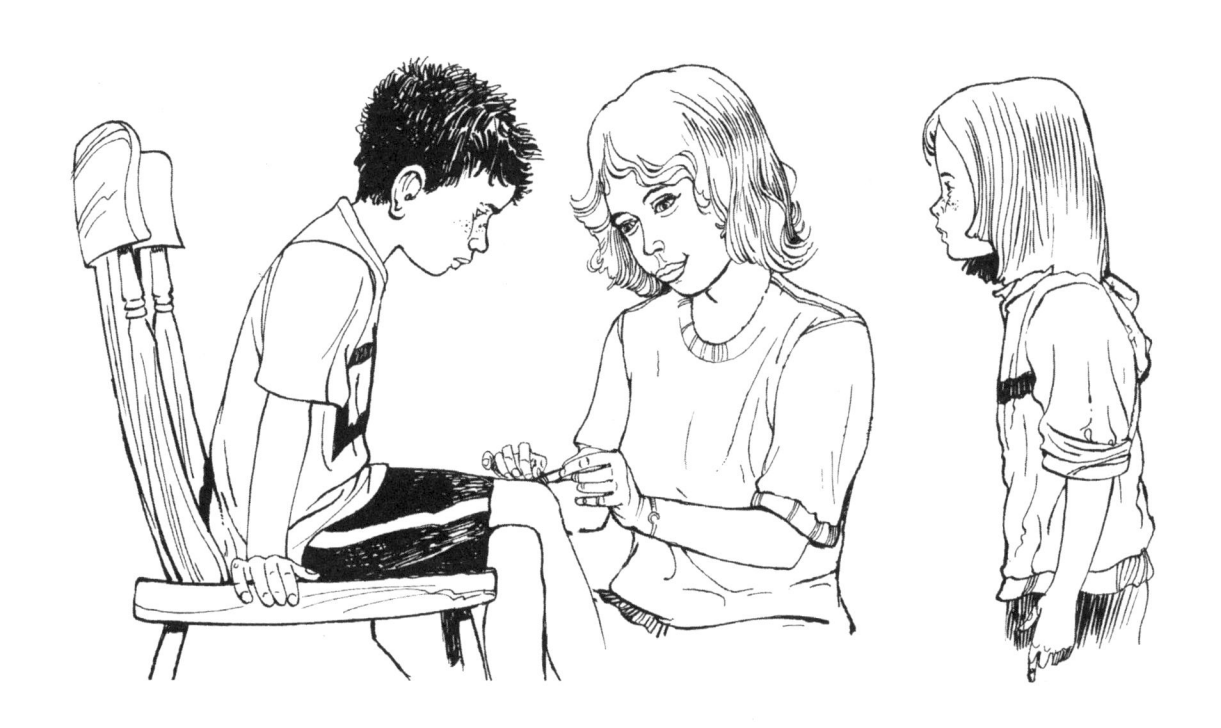

PRAYER: Lord Jesus, we thank you that you love us. Thank you for showing us when we don't love you. Help us to give over to you anything that would stop us loving you with all our hearts. Be with us we pray, for your sake. Amen.

ON GOD'S SIDE

Medals

Have you ever seen someone wear a medal? What kind of person would wear a medal? Athletes sometimes wear medals. But I want you to think about a different sort of medal. In the years 1939-1945 there was a terrible war in Europe and many people died. Many men and women did great and brave deeds – and because of their bravery they were awarded medals. There were many battles on the land, in the air, and on the sea during that time.

It is dangerous to be at war. What do you think these soldiers thought of just before they went into battle?

The Battle of Jericho

A long, long, time ago Joshua was getting ready to fight a battle against the city of Jericho. He was wondering how his army could defeat this great city. It was going to be a difficult job. Jericho was surrounded by a large, thick wall and there was no way in.

Suddenly, Joshua saw a man standing in front of him dressed for battle with a sword in his hand. If I had been Joshua, I might have turned and run in the other direction! But Joshua stayed to ask the man a question. He could see that he was a soldier. So he asked him, 'Are you on OUR side or are you on JERICHO'S side?'

It was a sensible question, wasn't it? The man was a warrior and he had a sword too. It was important to know whether he was on Joshua's side or whether he was on Jericho's side.

But guess what the man said? He said, 'No.'

READ: Joshua 5: 13–15

LESSON: Be sure that whenever Jesus calls you to follow him that you are on his side!

'Well,' Joshua thought, 'If you're not for Jericho and you're not for us, who are you for?'

This is what the soldier replied, 'I am the Captain of the Lord's army.'

Joshua should not have been asking the questions! The captain was there to find out whose side Joshua was on. Was Joshua on God's side or wasn't he?

Who is the Captain of the Lord's army? Jesus! So whenever you meet with Jesus don't say, 'Are you on my side or are you on their side?' Instead, listen to the question that he asks you, 'Are you on my side?'

Do you have an answer to that question? What would you say? Would you say, 'Yes! Jesus. I'm on your side'?

When you are on Jesus' side and you follow him it can be pretty tough going, like being in a battle. So, say to Jesus, 'I'm on your side.' Whenever Jesus calls you to be on his side, he will not only lead you – he will also protect you!

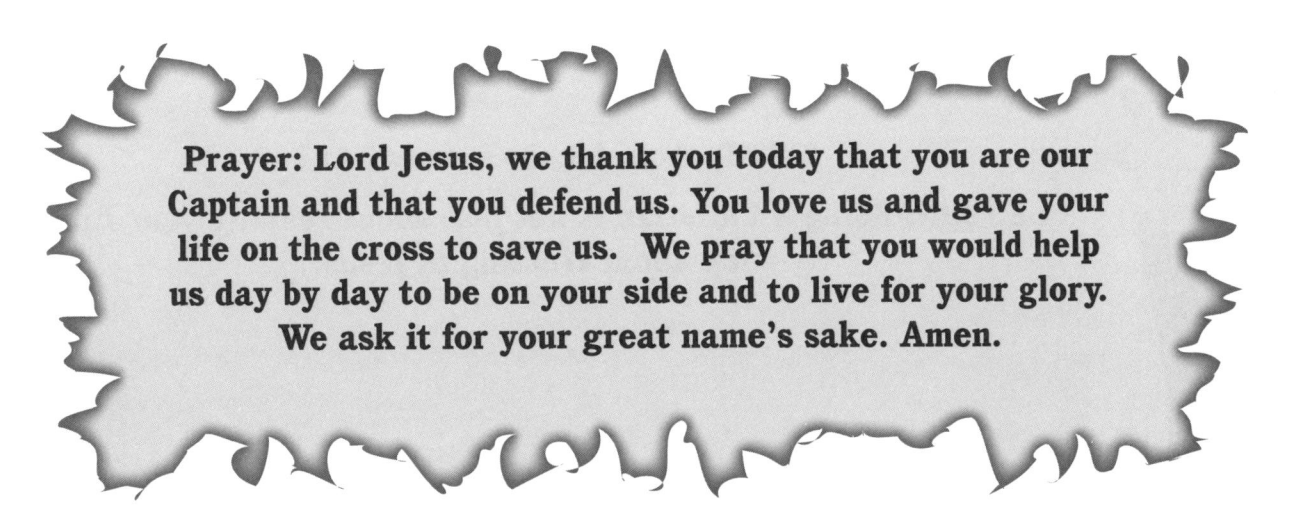

Prayer: Lord Jesus, we thank you today that you are our Captain and that you defend us. You love us and gave your life on the cross to save us. We pray that you would help us day by day to be on your side and to live for your glory. We ask it for your great name's sake. Amen.

PAUL AND BARNABAS

Some Nasty People

We are told in the Acts of the Apostles that some people began to get nasty with the Apostle Paul and his friend, Barnabas. Paul and Barnabas were telling them about Jesus. Does that seem strange? Sometimes when you start telling people about Jesus they become quite horrible.

The story of Paul and Barnabas reminds me of a time when I was sixteen years old. I hadn't been a follower of Jesus for all that long. I was really keen to tell others about him. I had a very good friend who was, I think, a little older than I was. He felt the same way I did. We both decided that we had to do something to tell people about Jesus.

Here is what we decided we would do.

We got some books about Jesus, and went to a part of our city where people really needed to hear about Jesus. We thought if we did it near home, somebody might try to stop us! So we went to a part of the city where nobody knew us. It was nerve-racking.

We got there and climbed up some stairs and knocked at a door. When the door opened there was an enormous man who towered above us! He was just a giant! He was huge! I said to him, 'We – we – we – we wondered if you would be interested in a book that would help you to know about Jesus and trust in him.'

The man got angry. His face began to go red. He pointed a finger in my face and said, 'If I ever see you and this son of yours ever again, I'll throw you down the stairs!'

READ: Acts 13: 1–3; Acts 14: 1–7

LESSON: Being a Christian is not just about reading your Bible - it's about trusting in Jesus.

I tried to smile at him! I didn't stop to tell him that the friend he had called my son was older than I was!

After the man had slammed the door in our faces we went back down the stairs. We remembered how the Lord Jesus had said, 'If anybody treats you really nasty because you've been trying to tell them about me, I will be with you. You'll have absolutely nothing to fear. I'll fill you with the joy they would have had if they had trusted in me.'

I was sad about what had happened, like Paul and his friends. But Jesus filled my heart with his joy.

Do you have friends who don't know very much about Jesus? I wonder if you could tell them about him. If anybody ever gets nasty with you, remember Jesus' promise. He has said that you'll have double joy because you're serving him!

PRAYER: Lord Jesus, we thank you that you have promised to be with us always. Please give us courage to speak about you and to say that we love you and trust you. We know that you died for us and we know that you're with us. We pray that you would help us to be your witnesses. For your name's sake. Amen.

WHO DO YOU WANT?

Who is Coming to Lunch?

Imagine it's lunchtime and there is an extra seat at the table with a knife and a fork and maybe a spoon. You say to Mum or to Dad, 'Who's coming to lunch today?'

Then Mum says to you, 'Anybody you want. You can have anybody you want to come to lunch today. Anybody famous, anybody from history that you've read about'.

What would you say to her? Who would you like to have?

Jesus Appears to the Disciples

For about six weeks after Jesus' crucifixion, the disciples kept laying an extra place at the table. If you had asked them who was coming to lunch – they'd have said 'Jesus.' How could this be if he had just died? Jesus had risen from the dead, and for weeks he kept turning up again. Why do you think he did this? He wanted to teach them more about what he had done.

Now if you had Jesus with you for lunch you'd have lots of questions to ask him. How did you walk on the water? How did you still the storm? The disciples would have had a lot of questions too. But Jesus was really preparing them for the time when he would leave to go back to his Father in Heaven.

There was one important lesson that Jesus wanted to teach them. Jesus had said a very strange thing to them before he died: 'It's going to be better for you that I leave you.'

READ: Acts 1:3–8

LESSON: When Jesus left this world to go to heaven he sent us His Holy Spirit to be with us forever.

How could it possibly be better for them if Jesus went? That's hard to understand, isn't it?

This is what Jesus taught them: 'I'm going to go away and then in my place I'm going to send you the Holy Spirit.'

Do you remember when Jesus was born, it was because of the work of the Holy Spirit? When Jesus was tempted he overcame the temptations through the power of the Holy Spirit. All the miracles and mighty deeds that Jesus did - he did in the power of the Holy Spirit. When he died on the cross, the Holy Spirit was with him, giving him strength so that he could go through the pain. And when he rose from the dead, the Bible tells us that the power of the Holy Spirit was at work.

So right from the moment that Jesus was just a tiny baby, all the way through his life the Holy Spirit had been with him. When it was finally time for him to leave his disciples, he said, 'I am going to give you the Holy Spirit who was with me for all of those years. He's going to come and live in your lives and because he has been with me all these years, it will be just like having me in your heart.'

So, when the Holy Spirit is in your life, it is like having Jesus with you, everywhere you go! This is absolutely amazing. The same Holy Spirit who helped Jesus has come to help us too.

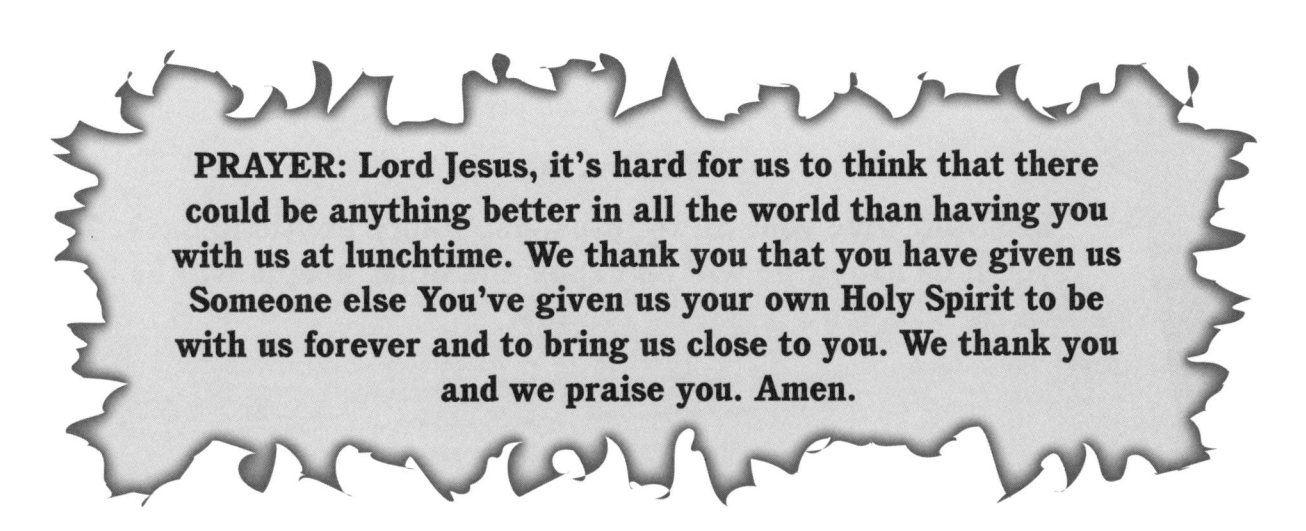

PRAYER: Lord Jesus, it's hard for us to think that there could be anything better in all the world than having you with us at lunchtime. We thank you that you have given us Someone else You've given us your own Holy Spirit to be with us forever and to bring us close to you. We thank you and we praise you. Amen.

MOTH BURGERS

Beware of the Moths

A whole family of moths must have been in my cupboard! I used to have some very nice socks – but these socks now have huge holes in them. Now they have ugly moth holes all over the toes! I left these socks at the back of my cupboard for far too long. Mr and Mrs Moth decided to pay a visit with all their baby moths.

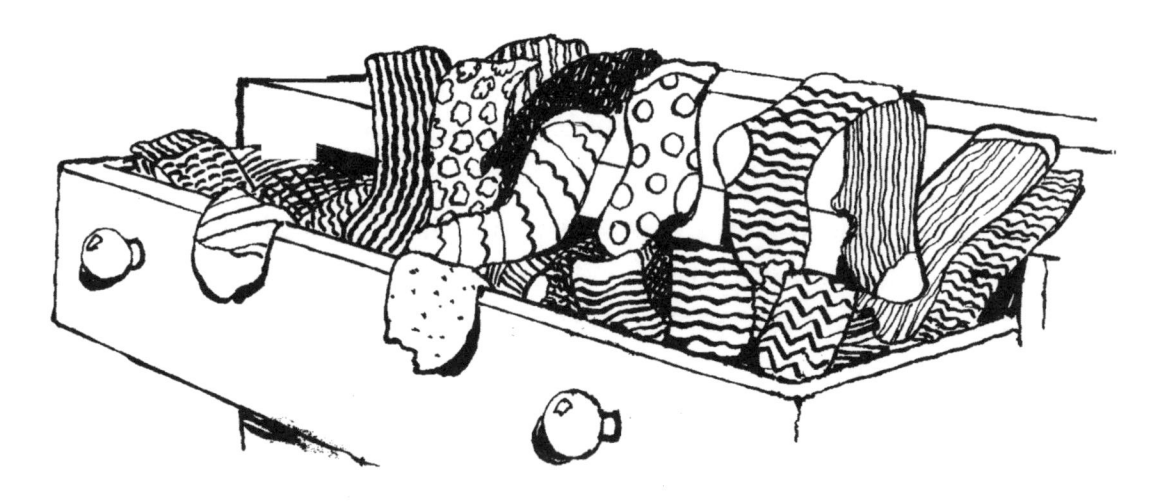

They must have thought that my socks looked like a tasty snack. Moths like to eat things like socks and sweaters. My socks must have seemed to them like Moth Burgers! Sock Burgers were on special offer – super size!

I think it would have been far better if I'd given my socks to someone who needed them. You see I had more socks than I needed. I had forgotten all about these extra ones.

READ: Luke 18: 1–30

LESSON: Give your all to Jesus, don't keep anything back. Then you'll be happy, he will be happy and other people will be happy too.

We can be like that, can't we? Even when we don't use something we don't want to give it to someone else. We say, 'It's mine and nobody else is getting it.'

James, the brother of our Lord Jesus, says 'When you don't give things to the Lord Jesus, but keep them for yourself, it's like putting your socks in the drawer. The moths will come and eat it all up!'

The Rich Young Ruler

If you are not prepared to give things to Jesus then you won't get any pleasure that lasts. I wonder if James knew about the young man that Jesus met one day. This young man had all kinds of good things. But he knew that it was only Jesus who could give him eternal life. So he asked Jesus what he needed to do in order to get eternal life.

Jesus said to him, 'Give away everything you've got to the poor then come and follow me.' Jesus was giving him a test.

The young man was very rich. He had lots of things stored away that he didn't really need. He wasn't using them for anybody else. They weren't doing anybody any good. He wanted to keep them for himself. When Jesus said, 'You come and follow me,' he couldn't leave his things. Even though these things would last only for a short time.

Jesus really liked this young man. He could give him eternal life. But the young ruler went away very sad. He just couldn't bring himself to give his things away – and so he could not hold on to Jesus.

What about you?

I wonder if you have something tucked away in your heart that you don't want to give to Jesus. Perhaps Jesus is saying to you, 'Give that thing to me so that we can use it together.' The safest thing to do is to give it all to Jesus. Then he'll be happy, you'll be happy and other people will be happy too!

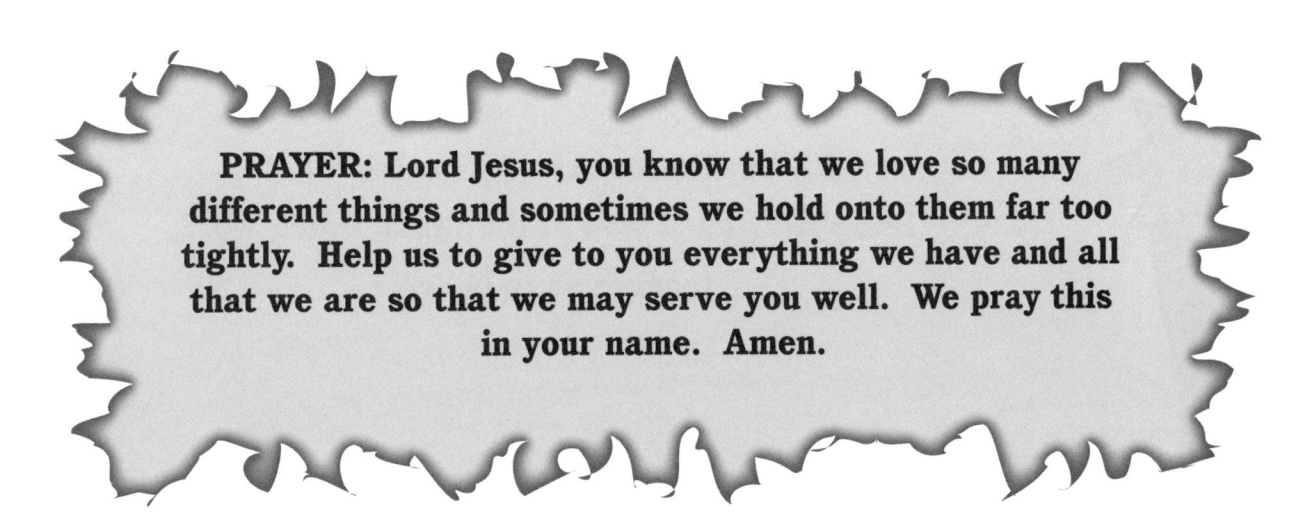

PRAYER: Lord Jesus, you know that we love so many different things and sometimes we hold onto them far too tightly. Help us to give to you everything we have and all that we are so that we may serve you well. We pray this in your name. Amen.

THE BIBLE

Expensive Bibles!

Jesus probably did not own a single book. He didn't even have a Bible. To own a Bible in Jesus' day you would have had to have lots of money. Bibles were so expensive! There was no printing or computers. People wrote things out slowly and paper cost a lot.

READ: Psalm 119: 99, Isaiah 50: 4.

LESSON: How a love of the Bible, God's Word, teaches us to be wise

One day some people who were jealous of Jesus said to him, 'How do you know so much when you don't have any books?' The answer was that Jesus had listened to the reading of the Bible, and had memorised as much of it as he possibly could.

Help From the Psalms

Psalm 119 was helpful to him. It is the longest Psalm in the Bible. It was written in a way so that Hebrew boys and girls could memorise it. The psalm was divided into sections. Each section began with a different letter of the Hebrew alphabet – starting at the first letter and then going through to the last letter. Each verse in the section then began with that same letter.

Psalm 119: 99 says, 'Because I love your Word, I know more than my teachers.' There were people in Jesus' day who had read all about God. But because Jesus trusted his Heavenly Father and thought about what God said he knew far more than them. In fact when Jesus was twelve years old, the teachers were amazed that he could answer questions about the Bible that they had been puzzled about for years.

In the Morning

Isaiah 50: 4 says something that was true of Jesus 'Every morning the Lord wakens me up and I listen to what he says.'

Jesus knew so much because he loved his Father and loved listening to him. Every morning he would be thinking, 'How can I do the things that my Father wants me to do?'

Here is a promise: Listen to what God says in his Word. Every morning wake up and wonder, 'How can I do what my Heavenly Father wants me to do today?' In a few years – it's a guarantee – you will know more than some of your teachers!

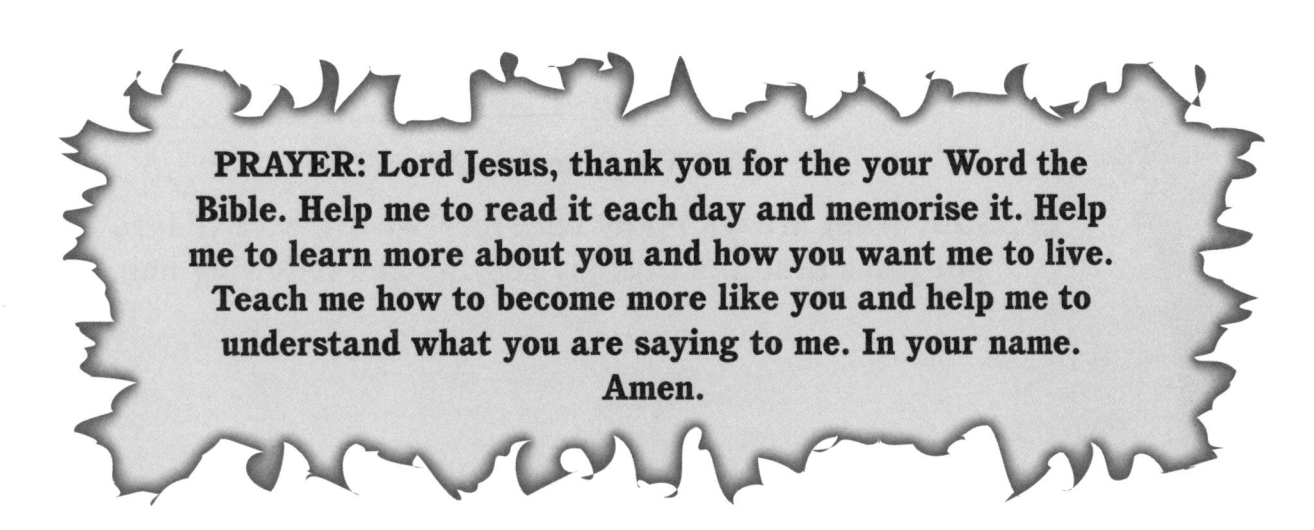

PRAYER: Lord Jesus, thank you for the your Word the Bible. Help me to read it each day and memorise it. Help me to learn more about you and how you want me to live. Teach me how to become more like you and help me to understand what you are saying to me. In your name. Amen.

Famous Last Words

Some Famous People

A very famous man died whose last words were 'Two eggs lightly poached'. What a way to die! The last words you hear from somebody are supposed to be words that you can remember. Well, here are some of my favourites. Remember these were the words people spoke just before they died.

Brigham Young

This man was not a true Christian. Here is what he said. His last words were, 'I feel better.' And then he died.

James Eades

This man was an engineer. He built things and he made things work. His last words were 'I cannot die. I've not finished my work.' But then he died.

Alfred Dupont

This gentleman was a very, very, very rich man. He said, 'Thank you, doctors. Thank you, nurses. I'll be gone in a few days.' And then he died.

READ: John 19: 28—37

LESSON: What are we really here for? We are here to love God, put Jesus first and to enjoy serving and following him.

Spencer Cole

Spencer Cole was a preacher. He had been preaching through the last book of the Bible. Just before he died he said, 'I should like to finish my exposition of the twenty-second chapter of Revelation.' And then he died. He never finished it – but he saw for himself what it describes!

All these last words have been written down by people who heard them. Last words are supposed to be words that people will remember. But first words can be important too!

Good Things to Remember

In the past many children used to learn the catechism. A catechism is a small book with lots of questions about God and lots of answers. Years ago somebody gave me one. The very first question and answer in my catechism was: 'What is the chief end of man?' Here is the wonderful answer: 'Man's chief end is to glorify God and to enjoy him forever.'

What does that mean? The question 'What is the chief end of man?' means 'What are we really here for?' The answer is 'To glorify God'. That means to love God, to put the Lord Jesus first, and to enjoy him. We are to enjoy loving him and serving him and following him.

I have a Bible that was given to me when I was a boy. I've kept it because in it I underlined the words that helped me to become a Christian: Jesus said, 'I am the Light of the World. Whoever follows me will not walk in darkness but will have the light of life.' These words are from John 8:12.

When I heard these words I began to trust in the Lord Jesus. So, the last words in this book are really first words: 'Glorify God and enjoy him forever.'

Follow Jesus because he said, 'I am the light of the world and if you follow me, you will never, ever, ever walk in darkness.' Will you do that?

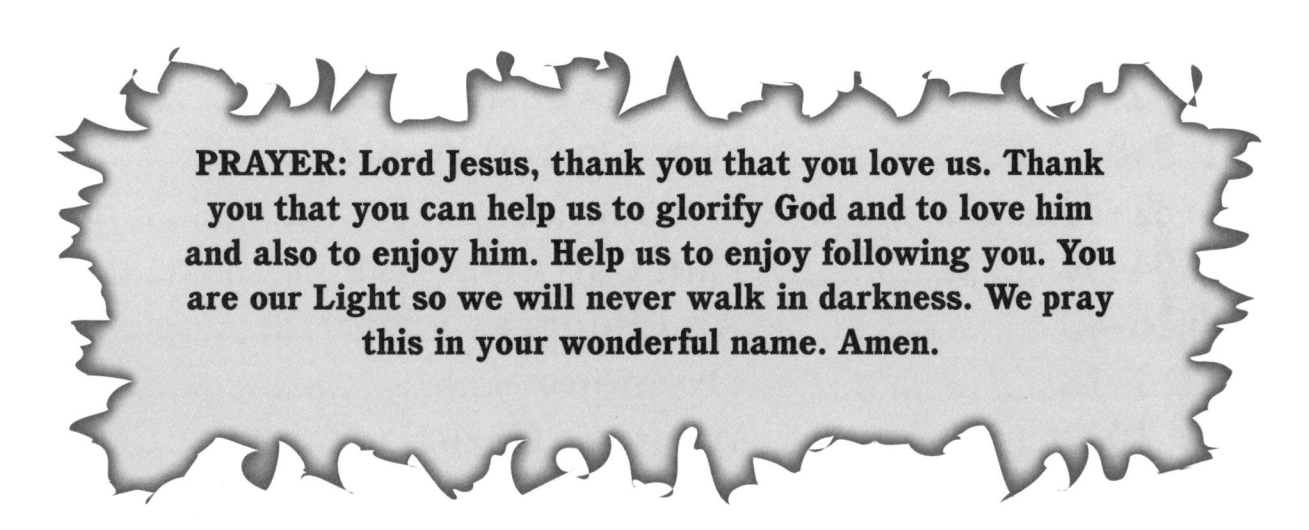

PRAYER: Lord Jesus, thank you that you love us. Thank you that you can help us to glorify God and to love him and also to enjoy him. Help us to enjoy following you. You are our Light so we will never walk in darkness. We pray this in your wonderful name. Amen.

Bible Reading Index

Old Testament
Passage   Lesson

Genesis 2: 7..........................* A Man Born Blind 44
Genesis 19: 1–26....................Don't Look Back 22
Genesis 20: 1–5......................Wisdom......................................18
Joshua 5: 13–15.....................Be On God's Side 48
1 Chronicles 11: 15–19...........* David's Big Three......................42
Psalm 10................................A Wicked Tongue 24
Psalm 119: 99........................* The Bible 56
Isaiah 50: 4............................* The Bible 56

New Testament
Passage   Lesson

Matthew 23............................The Heart 16
Luke 2: 41–52........................Growing Up.................................26
Luke 18: 1–30........................Moth Burgers..............................54
John 3: 1-21 ....Nicodemus..................................34
John 9: 1-12 ....* A Man Born Blind......................44
John 13: 1–30 ....Judas 46
John 14: 6 ....* Follow the Way 28
John 15: 18–19 ....Belonging to Jesus......................8
John 19: 28–37 ....Famous Last Words 58
Acts 1: 3–8............................Who Do You Want? 52
Acts 4: 32–36........................Nicknames 12
Acts 7: 54–59........................Paul Casts His Vote....................30
Acts 8: 26–40........................An Ethiopian Visitor....................36
Acts 11: 1–18........................Oxymoron 32
Acts 11: 19–26 ....What is a Christian?....................10

Acts 13: 1–3.............................* Paul and Barnabas.....................50
Acts 14: 1–7.............................* Paul and Barnabas.....................50
Acts 16: 16–40........................Paul in Trouble 40
Acts 24: 10–16........................* Follow the Way 28
Galatians 6: 12–18..................Get in a Time Machine 38
Philippians 2: 17 ....* David's Big Three 42
Hebrews 12: 1–2.....................Running the Race.........................6
James 2: 20–24 ....Just Do It! 20

* These stories have two bible readings

OTHER BOOKS BY SINCLAIR B. FERGUSON

Questions! Questions! Questions! Children are full of them. Where did I come from? What is God like? Is there only one God?

The Big Book of Questions and Answers is a family guide to the Christian faith. It contains a wealth of activities, prayers, and Bible references. This interactive resources material will bring families closer together as they learn about the Christian faith.

Sinclair B Ferguson is Senior Minister of The First Presbyterian Church of Columbia, South Carolina. He is also Distinguished Visiting Professor of Systematic Theology at Westminster Theological Seminary. He was formerly minister of St George's-Tron Church, Glasgow.

ISBN: 978-1-85792-295-0

Following on from the success of the original *Big Book of Questions and Answers,* this book tackles the many questions that children have about Jesus, including:

What was special about Jesus?
Why did Jesus heal sick people?
Why did Jesus have to die?
How can I give my life to Jesus?

An answer is given for each question, accompanied by a page of reading and a memory verse. To help the children take the message on board there are activities and suggestions for discussion. Prayers are also given to encourage them to bring every aspect of life to their Heavenly Father.

An invaluable tool for introducing children to Jesus and helping them to get to know him better, in an enjoyable and interactive way.

Short listed for 'Christian Children's Book of the Year'.

ISBN: 978-1-85792-559-3

We all love stories - can you ever have too many? There is no one better to hear about in a story than the greatest storyteller himself, Jesus. These stories will help you discover even more about him, his life, how he wants to get to know you.

In *The Big Book of Bible Truths 2* there are another twenty-seven stories that will teach you about what it means to belong to God's family. There are lots of different people to discover, including an architect and a master craftsman. You will also be able to work out what a revival is and if Jesus' mum ever got in a tizzy?

Sinclair tells many interesting stories that will teach you things you didn't know before. God, Jesus and You – what a team! Now that's a winning combination (no doubt about it!

There are illustrations throughout the book, so it's all set to be another of your family's favourites! Includes Extra Features: Bible reading; lesson summary; prayer.

ISBN: 978-1-84550-372-7

CHRISTIAN FOCUS PUBLICATIONS

Christian Focus | Christian Heritage | CF4K | Mentor

Christian Focus Publications publishes books for adults and children under its four main imprints: Christian Focus, CF4K, Mentor and Christian Heritage. Our books reflect that God's word is reliable and Jesus is the way to know him, and live for ever with him.

Our children's publication list includes a Sunday School curriculum that covers pre-school to early teens; puzzle and activity books. We also publish personal and family devotional titles, biographies and inspirational stories that children will love.

If you are looking for quality Bible teaching for children then we have an excellent range of Bible story and age specific theological books.

From pre-school to teenage fiction, we have it covered!

**Find us at our web page:
www.christianfocus.com**

CF4•K
*Because you're never
too young to know Jesus*